Local Wonders

Seasons in the Bohemian Alps

Ted Kooser

University of Nebraska Press

Lincoln and London

Publication of this book was assisted by a grant
from the Nebraska Arts Council.
Acknowledgments for previously published
material are on page xvii.
© 2002 by the University of Nebraska Press.
Manufactured in the United States of America
⊗
First Nebraska paperback printing: 2004

Library of Congress Cataloging in Publication Data
Kooser, Ted.
Local wonders : seasons in the Bohemian Alps/
Ted Kooser. p. cm. – (American lives series)
ISBN 0-8032-2751-5 (cloth : alkaline paper)
ISBN 0-8032-7811-x (paper : alkaline paper)
1. Garland Region (Neb.) – Description and tra-
vel. 2. Garland Region (Neb.) – Social life and
customs. 3. Garland Region (Neb.) – Rural con-
ditions. 4. Country life – Nebraska – Garland
Region. 5. Natural history – Nebraska – Gar-
land Region. 6. Seasons – Nebraska – Garland
Region. 7. Kooser,Ted. 8. Poets, American –
Nebraska – Biography. 9. Nebraska – Description and travel. 10. Nebraska – Social life and
customs. I. Title. II. Series.
F674.G37 K66 2002 978.2′3–dc21 2002017981

American Lives   Series editor: Tobias Wolff

For Jeff

When God wishes to rejoice
                the heart of a poor man,
He makes him lose his donkey
                and find it again.

Contents

Preface

Contrary to what out-of-state tourists might tell you, Nebraska isn't flat but slightly tilted, like a long church-basement table with the legs on one end not perfectly snapped in place, not quite enough of a slant for the tuna-and-potato-chip casseroles to slide off into the Missouri River. The high end is closest to the Rockies, and the entire state is made up of gravel, sand, and silt that ran off the front range over millions of years. Across this plain, the Platte River meanders side to side, like a man who has lost a hubcap and is looking for it in the high grass on both sides of the road. Its sluggishness as it presses forward to join the Missouri is expressed in patches of quicksand, at the bottom of which lie dozens of cautionary tales about toddlers who wandered away from family picnics and were sucked out of sight.

About seventy miles in from the eastern edge of the state is a north-south range of low hills known with a wink as the Bohemian Alps. These "alps," which in the late 1870s began to be settled by Czech and German immigrants from that region of central Europe once known as Bohemia, run about forty miles north and south and five or six miles east and west. No more than a hundred feet from bottom to top, they're made up of silty clay and gravelly glacial till with small red boulders that look like uncooked pot roasts. My wife Kathleen and I own two of those hills and the wooded crease between, where we have two dogs, a house, a barn, a chicken house, a corncrib made into a studio for art projects, and a shack where I read and write and look out over our small pond shining in the sun.

Our closest neighbors are coyotes, raccoons, opossums, badgers, field mice, fish, frogs, and birds. For birds we have flickers, blue jays, mourning doves, robins, wrens, red-bellied and downy woodpeckers, nuthatches, several kinds of sparrows, catbirds, brown thrashers, goldfinches, siskins, dickcissels, orioles, great horned owls, great blue herons, red-tailed hawks, northern harriers, turkey vultures, and, early each spring, the same pair of Canada geese that have come to our pond for ten years. They stay a couple of weeks but have never nested. But, as the Bohemians say, "A guest in the house, God in the house." We're glad for their annual visits.

People who know about such things tell me these gullies and the rises between were eroded out of a plain by water melting from a finger of the last glacier. That's their term, *finger*, and when a professional geologist, who usually uses terms like *Ordovician* and *anticline*, uses a word like *finger*, I know she's really trying to make me understand. But what I see in my imagination's eye is not a great ridge of melting ice but a real finger, an index finger, huge and wrinkled and white, with a dirty nail the size of a county, under the edge of which are packed all the little rocks that lie scattered in the fields where I live. I see not only that finger but also the whole last glacier, an enormous naked man who has caught his toes under the northern edge of Canada and fallen forward, flattening the continent. One arm is outstretched, and at the end of that arm is a dead snow-colored hand with a pointing finger. The finger points south, the direction in which he was trying to go. It is the direction many of the people who live in these hills would like to travel in mid-January, when the last glacier's death rattle blows down our necks.

With mediocre cropland – at best, thin, rocky topsoil – these alps were settled by people who fled Europe during the conflicts for ascendancy between Bohemia and Germany during the last quarter of the nineteenth century. The church was seen by many of the Czechs as another of their oppressors, and a sizeable number of these immigrants came to this country as freethinkers. Others have remained faithful Catholics.

The Slavic tribes had lived at the center of Europe for centuries, and it must have been hard to pack up and leave. One of their proverbs reads, "A horse has four feet, but yet it falters." By the end of the nineteenth century, however, the population of Bohemia was crowded, 315 people to the mile, and in the distant hills of Seward County, Nebraska, there were only a few families to the mile. The news got out. Their proverb says, "Tell it to the pig, and the pig will tell it to the boar, and the boar will tell it to the forest." They came in droves, with children, overcoats, and kettles.

In Bohemia, 65 percent were Czechs (including the Moravians) and

35 percent were Germans. They arrived in Nebraska in about the same proportions, and I'd guess the population of the Bohemian Alps is apportioned about the same today. They got here a little too late to claim the best land, but they accepted what they found and took good care of it. "As the thing is cut and sewn, so it must be worn," their saying goes.

In taverns and cafes in little towns like Loma, Dwight, Abie, and Bruno (formerly Brno, after the capitol of Moravia), you can hear older Czechs, now in their seventies and eighties, speaking their native language, but the old European card games of euchre and pinochle have been set aside in favor of pitch and hearts. The youngest descendants of the original settlers, sitting at other tables, may know a few Czech words but prefer to talk the hard yardage language of Nebraska football. They eat microwaved Tombstone pizza, burgers and fries. No *jaeternice*, spicy blood sausage, for them.

Old and young prefer the least expensive American beers – no pricey European pilsners bought in Lincoln – and I can attest from picking up litter that 98 percent of the cans thrown out along the road these days are Busch Lite. The other 2 percent are Mountain Dew, a modest gesture toward sobriety and a salute to the salubrious effects of caffeine.

Every summer, the little town of Dwight, a dozen miles north of my home, has a Czech festival, and young and old put on bright peasant costumes decorated with colorful embroidery. For a few dollars, you can buy a plate heaped with roast duck, kraut, and dumplings. At another festival in the town of Prague (pronounced *prāg*) the Czechs bake the world's biggest *kolache*, a doughy roll with a sweet filling of apricots, prunes, blueberries, figs, poppy seeds, or cherries. The world's biggest *kolache* is twice as big as the Nebraska governor's Lincoln Town Car and is baked in an insulated shed heated with gas burners till its tin walls shudder and ping. When the day is over, as the Bohemians say, "it is easy for the satiated man to fast."

And there are a few people who still cook thrifty European peasant meals for their families. A friend was at the meat counter in a grocery store looking at a display of pig feet and pig ears, and out of pure curiosity he asked a nearby shopper, a woman in middle age, how a person might go about cooking a pig's ear. "Oh," she said, with a little Czech accent, "I don't know how others do. I fry them up real crisp and then crumble them over my husband's oatmeal."

The Czechs who live in the alps, with few exceptions, are Republican, and their neighbors, the Germans, are also Republican. In Nebraska, a "conservative" state despite the farmers' longstanding dependence upon massive federal programs, the Democrats are just another kind of Republican. The few Democrats who manage to get elected to office talk the standard fiscal-conservative, tax-cutting, state's rights, welfare-baiting Republican line and would probably be members of the other party if everybody could fit on that side of the ticket. "Where sheep are lacking," say the Bohemians, "the goats are honored."

Our postal address is Garland, Nebraska, a village of about two hundred people. Garland used to be called Germantown. In 1918, when anti-German sentiment was at its most intense, Germantown went the way of *frankfurter* and *dachshund*, which became *liberty sausage* and *liberty dog*. According to local lore, a soldier named Garland was the war's first casualty from our area. He died not under fire in France but in the states, having been run over by a truck and then dying of a gangrenous toe. The town celebrated its name change with a huge bonfire.

Garland has a co-op elevator, two taverns that open at noon and stay open late, a coffee shop that opens early and closes by noon, a body shop, an auction house, and a handsome little Greek Revival bank with four fluted columns. The Germantown State Bank has been the resting place of fallen plaster and castoff implement parts since the bank went on holiday in 1933 and never came back. The banker was a respected man who tried, but "he who goes seeking other people's sausages often loses his own ham."

If it's Friday night when you get to Garland, and you're hungry from the drive, you can get a slab of prime rib or an open-faced carp sandwich, baked potato or hash browns, and an iceberg lettuce salad garnished with a couple of saltines in cellophane envelopes. And you can pick up a six-pack of Busch Lite for the road.

Go a mile and a half straight north from the bank, turn east, and follow that road along the ridge for a quarter mile. From there, you can get a great view of the alps rolling away toward Loma and Valparaiso – soft green pastures dotted with red cedars; shadowy groves of burr oak, cottonwood, red elm, and hackberry; fields of corn and soybeans with rows that wrap around the curving hills. Grant Wood's paintings of hillside fields in Iowa could be taken to depict this landscape.

Legend has it that during the Civil War, a man from Missouri drove his pigs north to keep them from being taken by the Confederate soldiers. In the dense oak grove you see just north of the ridge road, his pigs feasted on acorns and frolicked in the underbrush. When the war ended, their owner was unable to drive them out, and though he went home to Missouri, they stayed in Nebraska. Though most of the early settlers had been discouraged by the rocky soil and severe weather of the Bohemian Alps, the pigs survived the hard winters and prospered. They were our first settlers, and for many years there were sightings of wild pigs north of Germantown.

Turn right at the first corner, go three-quarters of a mile, and you'll be at our gate. At the top of our lane, in that big tin mailbox with its flag flipped up to catch the attention of our route carrier, are the pages of this book, carefully wrapped in clean butcher paper and tied with grocery string, with proper postage in American flag stamps purchased from Iris Carr, the Garland postmistress, who counted the change back twice to be sure she hadn't cheated me. She's been known to send out a handwritten sticky note thumbed to the rest of the mail: "Ted and Kathy, your newspaper did not come today. Iris." That yellow note is just one of the thousand reasons we like it here.

The Bohemians say, "The cat makes sure whose chin it may lick," and I caution you that though this book is about the Bohemian Alps, you'll find me wandering off the track from time to time to talk about my family and the past. As my neighbors would say, "Sheltered by a wall, even an old man becomes courageous."

Acknowledgments

First, to Kathleen, with love and gratitude. Next, to my friend of nearly forty years, Laura Casari, for her help with the manuscript. To Carol and Leonard Nathan, dear friends and fellow writers, for their persistent encouragement. To Frank Brown, counselor and friend. And to these people to whom I owe my life, my dentists and doctors: Alan Korte, Paul Sheridan, Eric Rippert, David Cohen, Bill Lydiatt, Dina Howell-Burke, and Scott Rasmussen.

A few parts of this book have been published elsewhere. The section about weed spraying was substantially rewritten from its original appearance in the anthology *Sacred Trusts: Essays on Stewardship and Responsibility*, edited by Michael Katakis (San Francisco: Mercury House, 1993). Reprinted by permission. The section about my father's hands was first published in *Nebraska English Journal* and later included in my long essay, "Lights on a Ground of Darkness," published in *Great River Review*. The remembrance about making Christmas bows in my father's store was first published in *Nebraskaland*. The section about *Lentil* was published as "Riding With Colonel Carter" as a chapbook from Sandhills Press. The section about the phantom book, "King, Dog of the North," first appeared in *North Dakota Quarterly*.

The Bohemians say, "He who wants to know himself should offend two or three of his neighbors." I hope I have not done so.

Spring

*The swallow carries spring
on its wings.*

Fat slides of snow plop from the wet tin roofs of turkey sheds, and it's suddenly spring, the barnyard air in compartments of warm and cold, blue in the shadows and yellow over the pooled wheel ruts in the sunny pigpens.

I like to get outside and paint pictures in the early spring. I suppose it's my way of trying to be a tulip, pushing my way out of the tight white bulb of winter and opening a little color against the drabness.

I've converted my '92 Mercury Topaz into a rolling art studio so I can paint wherever I can park, and in all weathers. I built a small plywood table over the passenger's seat for my palette, paints, and brushes, and a Masonite easel that fastens over the steering wheel. For a week I've been out making watercolor sketches and was blessed to observe the first greens coming on in the roadside ditches. On the first day everything was the dusty deer-hide brown of late winter. On the second day I could begin to see traces of green in the sunnier spots. And by the third, there was green everywhere. Though I'm an amateur painter and my color mixing isn't good enough to perfectly capture this transition, my first day's sketch, of a field of corn stubble, looks like late winter, and the third day's, of a couple of big hay bales in the shelter of some trees, looks like early spring. That's accomplishment enough for a Sunday painter in his sixties.

While I was parked by the road, a farmer pulled out of the lane to a farmhouse about a quarter of a mile away and drove slowly toward me in his pickup. When he got up beside me, he stopped, rolled down his window, leaned out, and asked if I needed any help. He looked to be about my age. "No," I said, "I'm just painting a picture." I could tell by the look on his face that he'd never run into anything quite like that before, but he just said "Oh," as if it happened every day, and rolled up his window, tight enough to seal in his sense of the way things ought to be. Then he drove to the next corner, turned around, came past me again, and turned back into his lane.

3

The seasons change so quickly. By the end of the week there were robins everywhere, a few early mourning doves, and this morning I saw two handsome meadowlarks on a power line. The ants have been back for a couple of weeks from wherever they go during the cold months, and hundreds patrol our kitchen. We'll try to keep the honey and molasses out of reach and a couple of those pillbox ant traps blocking their trails until they get tired of stepping around them and move back outside.

Two inches of snow during the night and, by the stoop, five blind tulip bulbs lie under a fastness of white, their long green ears sleepily hearing me knock snow from my boots. Some evening, weeks from now, coming home tired and preoccupied, I'll find them waiting, huddled beside the doorstep, boldly lifting their red wooden bowls.

For the wedding of his daughter, a rich man who lived near here once ordered every white tulip in the United States. By plane, by train, by refrigerated truck, thousands of tulips arrived in Nebraska, nestled in tissue. Those tulips were like a vast beach gleaming with shells. Great tides of happiness washed over the wedding and vanished. Long stems drank up the names of the guests, and the gifts and good wishes poured into the silent white cups of the petals. Can we remember the bride or the groom? No, we remember the tulips. They were the story.

It's very cold today with a fierce wind blowing drifts of snow across the country roads. I've been outside a couple of times in my parka, wearing a cap my father crocheted about thirty years ago. It looks like a standard stocking cap, but the brim has been rolled up and sewn to the crown so you can't unroll it over your ears, and there's an odd little ridge that runs from front to back that helps it fold flat like a purse. It may have started out to be a purse. I suspect he discovered its probable use as he knotted along. He'd recently retired from his job as a department store manager and was trying to find things to do with his hands. He made two of these caps, this white one and one in brown, and then went on to something else. I've forgotten what that was.

Though you can't see the strand of sentiment I've threaded through the turned up edge, it's there all right, tying the present up against the past with the strength of piano wire or catgut. And this cap keeps warm a head that holds a vivid picture of my father sitting in his chair with the floor lamp pulled close, busy making this cap or purse or pocket or whatever it seemed at first to be.

Mind you, not making a cap for me, but something for himself. He's making it so as to learn from making it. He's accepting a gift he's giving himself. Only later will it occur to him to present it to me, pretending he'd been thinking of me all along. But I don't mind; to make a cap, a sock, or mitten – to take a ball of dime store yarn and knit or crochet it into some useful thing – is an act of generosity. Someone is all the warmer for its presence in the world.

Bound in an ill-fitting sweater knitted by an aunt, or squeezed into a handmade shirt whose collar points are tapered long and out of fashion, you can speed straight into the past, lit by a floor lamp with a yellow shade. There must be stocking caps all over the world that, when you pull them on, sweep you to another time.

There ought to be an annual holiday for the celebration of things like my cap. We could wear handmade clothes and parade through second-hand stores all over America, pausing to praise the neatly sewn blouses that didn't quite fit, the knitted neckties stretched out of shape, and the corduroy jumpers children grew out of before they could ever try them on. And at the front of each column of marchers, someone could carry a banner reading "Thank You, Thanks For Everything."

The sidewalks in Lincoln have been slippery since last weekend's snowstorm, and a light snow that fell during the night has made them even more dangerous. I was there this morning to run errands, and people were walking deliberately, heads down, buttocks clenched. They frowned at their shoes as if they required supervision, as if they might suddenly set out on a new track, the way amoebas move under a microscope.

When I was a boy, I attended ballroom dancing lessons in the Methodist church basement, and the old janitor, Mr. Coffey, would sprinkle dance wax on the floor. Dance wax was a pale yellow dust that made the floor more slippery. It was supposed to assist your feet in lurching

5

less awkwardly through the fox-trot, buttocks clenched, a challenging grown-up entertainment we were being taught. When doing the fox-trot, you locked your partner in a Greco-Roman hold, stared over her shoulder toward the nearest exit, and with sweating hands shoved her around the edges of invisible squares on the floor. All this to a one-two-three-four rhythm that you tried to count out without moving your lips. The waltz, which we were also learning, was based on similar but more diaphanous squares. Their sides seemed longer, and their phantom grid work slid away underfoot like floes of ice in a swirling river.

At the end of the dancing lessons there was a party at which we showed off what we'd learned. Our parents attended. We fox-trotted and waltzed and looked our very best and then had cups of punch, a sugary red concoction with lots of maraschino cherries. Billy Stoever and I had a contest to see who could drink the most, and as I left the church, I threw up in a snowbank just outside the door. We had not a single flake of snow the rest of the winter, and the stain was indelible, bright pink, dotted with small chunks of cherry. It was right on the way to school, too, and everybody who walked past that snowdrift would say, with a cautionary nod of the head, "That's where Teddy Kooser threw up at the end of the ballroom dancing lessons."

Thaw. It starts with the sun's thin breath on the face of a stone that's been trussed in a harness of wire and hung in the tines of a hay rake, the white chalk from the rock's cold face a powder that clouds the glistening film welling up out of the pores, bathing the rock and the wire with a sheen that seeps and flashes as moisture eases slowly down, condensing into a single drop, a shimmering orb that mirrors the world on a morning in March: the pale blue sky with spit curls of cloud, an old barn, gray and swaybacked, a yellow house with winter sheets snapping on a clothesline, a white cat sunning herself on a hay bale pushed up for warmth against the cold foundation.

That one drop trembles, elongates, and falls to a troughlike blade of grass where it tumbles – a quicksilver ball – down into the shadows on the floor of the pasture. And there a musical trickle gathers its strength, droplet by droplet, putting its will to assembling a powerful muscle of

6

water, the color of coffee with cream, a runnel of cold brown force that can push itself over the lips of cut and rut with a muddy gleam on its swollen leafy skin.

Spring
Summer
Autumn
Winter

Soon you can hear it everywhere, the sound of water trickling, shearing from pebble and hill, the lock of winter slipping, the chill drip-drop, drip-drop of what seems to be all the world's water, running, feeling its way up out of the sockets of tree roots, spilling from roof and sill, from every tilt and crease and lip and corner, till the steep black creek banks soften with winter's easing.

On the water's shining surface, ice that is mealy, pitted, and broken turns like broken eggshells, each piece pushing up over another or sliding down out of sight in the greasy foam. With a sound like a sigh, a high bank shears from a field and slips in, carrying sod and stone and mouse hole, waving the whip of a willow tree – a nest woven of grass in its top – and then another tree topples, the flood chewing off chunks of cornfield, beanfield, lane, and pasture, washing in under the popping roots and the scuffed red elbows of trees, till a whole grove shudders, leaning, sweeping its freshly budded branches – burnt red bud of the maple, bullet-hard bud of cottonwood – out over the turning, rolling surface.

Creek into river now, hulks of trees floating far out in the channel, black mud shearing from root balls, a turtle clinging, blinking, dazzled by sun on the molten brown glass, a sandpiper riding a wooden crate wedged into the branches, lifting one leg, then the other, looking downstream where a round wooden pig shed turns, roof-deep, all ringed with yellow foam.

And miles behind the flood, the stone from which the first drop oozed and shone and fell, hangs drying in its harness of wire.

*

In every town with a couple hundred people, there are at any given moment of a sunny day in early spring at least a half dozen people cleaning out their car sheds. That 3 percent of the population probably holds true in communities large and small across America, but it is much easier to imagine in a village like Garland, where the only people you see moving at ten on a weekday morning in early March are the fellow who tends

7

the grain elevator, standing outside and enjoying the sun while he waits
for a gravel truck to drive over his scale, and a few women with brooms,

whisking about in the cool blue shadows of their garages.

I prefer *shed* to *garage* as a nod to my maternal grandfather, whose
birth predated the automobile by about thirty years and who preferred
car shed, having grown into manhood comfortable with the word *shed*
before it occurred to anybody to roll a car into one. The first car sheds
were just that, of course, small buildings in which cars were *shaded*,
shade being at the root of *shed*. These little buildings stood apart from
houses, just as a pig shed did.

But the Northern European hankering to bring the family's farm animals into one end of the house began to nudge at the tinkering, restless
part of the American soul, and within a few years after the introduction
of the automobile, car sheds were being built as attachments to houses.
After all, the husband might have told his wife, why not share a common wall and spare the lumber? And besides, a car is just as much a part
of the family as is a milk cow. Today no one would think of building a
house without building on a room or two for the family automobiles,
many of which have been given names, like cows. And their own private
entrances too.

So, on a day like this, when the family Ford has been driven out to
feed in the tender spring pasture of commerce, there are people at home
cleaning out its stall. Tomorrow, all up and down side streets, we'll see
cartons of debris set out for the trash hauler.

I too am getting the urge. Our car shed has accumulated a lot of junk
during the winter, and I want to get rid of it before it becomes a permanent part of the structure, which can happen. Things left too long in car
sheds have a way of becoming encrustations, like barnacles. They take
on a uniform color and begin to look like part of the building.

A couple of years ago I was invited to an outdoor barbeque at a farm
about twenty miles from home. The man holding the party worked in
the city and was renting the farmhouse. The landowner had leased the
cropland for farming, but no one was using the barn and other farm
buildings. I took a stroll around the place and spent quite a while standing by myself in a small dilapidated car shed a few yards behind the

house. It had been used not only for shading a car but also as a workshop, and there were lots of interesting old hand tools hung on nails. They had been unused and unmoved for so long they were becoming part of the walls. Everything was the same color, a warm brownish gray. The wooden handles of the hammers – ball-peen and mallet and claw – were the same color as their steel heads. The blade of the sickle was the same as its handle. Cans of nails and jars of nuts and bolts were all the same dull hue. An old fly net for a draft horse hung on one wall. Once leather brown, it too had turned gray.

This wasn't just the result of field dust that had collected over the years but of that dust combined with the timeless shade and stillness, the cool motionless shadows that resisted the busy workaday light which stood beyond the open door. All those tools, once so different in shape and color and purpose, all those cartons of spark plugs and odd nuts and bolts were, through their neglect, becoming one homogeneous mass of gray: wood, steel, rubber belts, cardboard, and straps of leather. It occurred to me that unless somebody cleans out that building, there will come a time when it can no longer be cleaned. Everything will have become inextricably woven together, like a bird's nest, like the life experiences of the very old, buried in cartons and loose gray coils of memory, where things take on the color of the singular mind in which they lie unwanted and unmoved.

So before my coil of clothesline rope begins to weave its way through the spokes of my bicycle, I'd better get out my broom. Besides, it is always a pleasure to stand in the cool shade of a dirty car shed and look out into a busy spring day.

Our new pup, Alice, and I have been out digging a posthole. Alice came from the humane society in Lincoln, and they told me the people who left her there called her Café au lait. Name a dog Café au lait in Garland and people will start talking. So we named her Alice, as in "My Sweet Little Alice Blue Gown." She's black and white, probably part cow dog, part Dalmatian, and part greyhound.

It's a cool overcast morning, so still I can hear the beeping of the county road grader, driven by my neighbor Lindsay French, as he backs up and turns around at the intersection three-quarters of a mile away. Two pairs of yellow-shafted flickers have been noisily arguing over one hole in a dead elm tree in the draw that's west of the garden, although they have my old barn with a dozen big holes already drilled in it.

Spring
Summer
Autumn
Winter

Last spring I tore out a chicken wire fence that had been around the garden for a dozen years and had been woven through and through with wild plum saplings, weeds, and tough grass. I tried to grow some vegetables without the fence, but the rabbits ate everything. By fall there was nothing above the horizon but two bare Brussels sprouts stalks that looked like walking sticks somebody had stuck in the ground and walked off without. The deer ate those this past winter. So I'm building a new fence.

I knew Alice would enjoy the outing, and she does, furiously digging right next to the hole I am making, trying to see how fast she can run in big circles without losing her footing on the dewy grass, and eating a few dead leaves, and then coughing them up. She also discovered that a small clump of sod makes a great plaything: you can toss it into the air, catch it, and shake the bejesus out of it, then run in a big circle with your tongue hanging out. The world is Miss Alice's oyster.

Working with a two-handled posthole digger is heavy exercise for the back and shoulders, so heavy that I stop halfway to have a cup of coffee and write a letter to an actor friend who lives along the Hudson River in New York and who, I imagine, is this morning sitting at a window looking down at the river while her three year old runs in circles like Alice. My pup falls asleep on the porch while I am writing about her, tired of being watched with such interest and love.

I tell my friend about our other dog, Buddy, an English pointer who at fourteen or fifteen years of age (he was a stray and we don't know his birth year) is so arthritic he lies motionless most of the day, sleeping or with his eyes just open enough to see if Alice is going to pounce on him again. She wants him to play and doesn't give up easily. She thinks he's a large rubber squeak toy. We've given him Ascriptin and steroids and are now trying a human arthritis medicine you can buy over-the-counter. It makes us feel better even if it doesn't help him much. I lie down on the rug next to him at least once a day and rub him all over and stick my

10

nose in his ear. His big paws smell like years of hard running, like a hayfield in sunlight. This is a dog who once killed badgers and raccoons and who ran with the coyotes.

Nebraska has three cities: Omaha and its suburbs, with over a half million people; Lincoln, with a little over two hundred thousand; and Grand Island, with about fifty thousand, which in some states would be considered a town. There are a number of towns with several thousand and hundreds of little villages like Garland that have survived from the days when you didn't want to be more than a dozen round-trip miles from a trading center, because that was about as far as you could push a team and wagon in one day. The rest of the state is a vast grassy preserve set aside for those of us who like to be left alone.

In the early 1980s, when my wife and I bought our property in the Bohemian Alps, the area had not yet been discovered by the developers in Lincoln, about twenty miles east of us. Our nearest neighbor in that direction was almost two miles away; to the west, a quarter of a mile; to the south, a half mile; and to the north, nearly a mile. Only on the coldest, stillest nights could we hear one of our neighbors' dogs barking.

Though we own only sixty-two acres, we had a couple hundred acres adjacent to us that we hiked as if it were our private park. In the past couple of years, the man who owned that property divided it into expensive twenty-acre lots, and someone has just built a big showy house on a hilltop right across our north property line, about three hundred yards from our house. Though we live on an old farmstead sheltered among trees in a valley, we can't avoid looking at this new house when we glance out our upstairs windows. I suppose they built where they did for the sunsets and sunrises, but soon their view to the east will be interrupted, because another family has bought a hilltop about a hundred yards away and will be building their own house there within the year. The two families will have to draw their blinds at night and listen to each other's screen doors slam just as they did in the city.

I trust in the Bohemian saying, "He who places his ladder too steeply will easily fall backward."

The telephone rang while I was down by the barn hanging a new bird-house from one of the supports on the windmill. I ran to the front porch,

Spring

Summer

Autumn

Winter

snatched up the extension, said "Hello," and a very small voice said a two-syllable something that turned up on the end like a question.

"Hello?" I said.

"Donnie?" she said, a little more clearly, in a small and uncertain voice. I could tell by that one word that I was hearing a widow in her seventies or eighties, living alone in a house she's lived in for forty years, calling her son to ask for help with some errand. It was a polite don't-let-me-impose voice, within a hair's breadth of being the voice of my late mother, and I was within a hair's breadth of being Donnie, or Don, as he'd probably prefer to be called by people other than his mother. There wasn't a bit of urgency in that word, "Donnie?", just a gentle little nudge. I was immediately ready to go for my jacket and car keys. Donnie and I were about to be tested.

How well I remember running small errands for my mother, taking her carefully written lists to the HyVee: "Two bananas if ripe. One loaf of white bread, store brand. Use coupon. One box of apricot Jell-O. Coupon for Jell-O." I fixed the stopper in her toilet tank, so the water wouldn't trickle any of her money away, and repainted the sill of the living room window, where she sat in her red upholstered armchair and looked out at the world. Sometimes there were errands that didn't really have to be done but were, I sensed, invented to give me something to do. I miss all that. I miss my mother. My sister, who lived in the same city as mother and who selflessly ran a thousand errands for every one I ran, must miss her too. It was Judy who stood in endless lines of old people on senior discount day at the drugstore, who drove Mother from one side of town to the other on the days the CDs matured so that Mother could take advantage of the best interest rate, even if it was only a quarter of a percent higher.

"No," I said, the start of a lump in my throat. "My name is Ted Kooser." Without a moment's hesitation I knew my caller was someone to whom you could give your whole name and never regret it.

"Oh, I'm sorry," she said, "I must have gotten the wrong number." And she promptly hung up. The receiver was suddenly hollow and light in my hand.

12

I hope Donnie was at home this morning and could drop whatever he was doing. If she wants to call me back, she knows my name and can find me in the book. I'd be happy to jump in the car and drive right over.

Spring
Summer
Autumn
Winter

.❧

The other evening, as I left our neighbors' house after checking in with their dear old golden retriever, Buffy – they're traveling – I saw, near a full moon, which was just then rising, a moondog, a flare of moonlight like a small section of a rainbow. I had never seen a moondog before, and it made me very happy. It was the transparent blue of a gas flame and stood in the sky about four degrees south of the moon.

And about a month ago, a mile east of our house, I saw my first bobcat. I came over a rise in my pickup, and it stood at the edge of the road about fifty yards ahead. It had its back arched and its legs bunched up as if it were playing with something, springing upon it and dancing away in the manner of cats, and I suppose it had caught a mouse or vole. It looked up when it heard my truck on the gravel and in a split second vanished into the weeds.

I delight in the things I discover right within reach. At sixty-one years of age, I have seen, within a short distance from my house, my first moondog and my first bobcat. Sue, who owns the golden retriever, told me she'd recently seen a fox. I have lived in the country for sixteen years and have yet to come upon a fox, though I have seen dozens of coyotes. I have since been squinting into the distance, hoping to see the same brushy tail she saw raised, and the fine red winter coat and the black eyes looking back.

To be happy, according to Webster, is to be favored by luck or fortune, and the first syllable of happiness, hap – with its luckiness, its chanciness, its sudden surprises – is a source of much delight in my life.

I am a disgruntled and miserable traveler. I don't like to be away from home. Travel and travail come from the same root, you know, and are for me synonymous. There is, of course, some hap in travel: you might walk through Mad Ludwig's castle in Bavaria and happen upon something unexpected, maybe a kangaroo mouse scampering along a cold corridor dragging a shred of toilet paper. But most travel, as we think of it – going somewhere to experience something – seems to me to be pretty predictable, a disciplined, highly structured, forced march toward something you can store in a logbook of things once seen and done. Carrying heavy luggage too. There can't be a whole lot of hap in flying to Europe to visit castles on the Rhine, nor could there have been much hap for the men who landed on the moon; they knew pretty much what they were going to find. If they'd seen a fine red fox standing on a rise in the distance, well, then that might have made them truly happy.

Spring
Summer
Autumn
Winter

Happiness, like hap, is where you find it. This morning Alice showed me a wet gray feather she'd found somewhere and gummed a little and brought into the glassed-in porch where she sleeps. The feather's shaft was marigold yellow. She had navigated the flap on the dog door without dropping this damp little piece of hap and was delighted. As was I.

Wild plums grow everywhere along the roadsides in our part of the country, each thicket originally started by some bird pausing on a fence wire just long enough to deposit a plum pit coated with a dollop of rich lime. The lines of plum bushes grow eight to ten feet high, interweaving their thorny branches, and in winter they resemble a great blue-black caterpillar crawling along the road. And in fact they *are* crawling, spreading by persistent little suckers that creep in every direction. Road work on one side and field work on the other keep the plum bushes confined to the ditches, but in spring, at the edge of every plowed field, you can see their broken, searching shoots, split open and stripped of their bark by the plowshare.

Often these thickets run for a quarter mile or more without a break, and they provide almost impenetrable cover for pheasants, quail, field mice, rabbits, beer cans, tumbleweeds, whiskey bottles, wild turkeys, Styrofoam hamburger boxes, and those batlike scraps of black plastic that one sees caught up on twigs everywhere, having been torn by the prairie wind from haystacks or silage heaps miles away. If Br'er Rabbit were to be miraculously swept up and transported from the Deep South onto our prairies, he would immediately recognize a plum thicket to be the perfect briar patch in which he could quickly hide from Br'er Fox (and, in Nebraska, from Br'er Coyote too).

From mid-April into early May, depending upon the lateness of spring, the plum thickets are in bloom. Waves of foamy white break along the roads and at the margins of the woods, contrasting with the dusty greens of the warming fields. The perfume of the wild plum is strong and intoxicating, and the thickets hum with bees. A sprig in a glass of water will fill an entire house with a delicious fragrance that will make you long for something you thought you had forgotten. The blossoms last only a week or so, then they begin to shrivel, turn pink, and soon they are gone, taking a piece of your heart with them. Then the leafing out follows – a bright green spatter along the dark twigs.

A late frost sometimes ruins the blossoms, and several years can pass between bearings. When things go well, the plums ripen in mid-August, the month called by the Lakota *Kan'tas'a wi*, meaning "red plum moon." Under the dusty red skins, the fruit is fleshy and yellow and can be cooked down into delicious preserves, distilled into delicate amber jellies, and fermented into a sweet pink wine. They are free for the picking.

Two books by Kelly Kindscher, *Edible Wild Plants of the Prairie* and *Medicinal Wild Plants of the Prairie* (Lawrence: University Press of Kansas, 1987 and 1992), tell a lot about wild plums. Kindscher says the Indians pitted and dried the fruit for their winter stores (though George Catlin noted in 1837 that the Indian children ate them from the bushes by the handful even while they were still green). William Clark of the Lewis and Clark expedition would have seen them still green when in July of 1804 he looked down upon the Nemaha valley in southeastern Nebraska:

> I had an extensive view of the Serounding Plains, which afforded one of the most pleasing prospect ever beheld, under me a Butifull River of Clear Water of about 80 yards wide Meandering thro: a leavel and extensive meadow, as far as I could See, the prospect much enlivened by the fiew Trees and Srubs which is bordering the bank of the river and the Creeks & runs falling into it, The bottom land is covered with Grass of about 4 and 1/2 feet high, and appears as leavel as a smoth surfice, the 2nd bottom is also covered with Grass and rich weeds & flours, interspersed with copses of Osage Plumb.

Wild plums were so useful as food and medicine that when the Pawnee were relocated to Indian Territory, they took dried plums with them and started new bushes from the pits. At digs all across the plains, archeologists have found plum pits, some of them more than a thousand years old. The Omaha gathered the springy twigs and used them for brooms.

They boiled the bark of the roots for an abrasions treatment. The Teton Dakota made painted wands from wild plum sprouts and fastened offerings to them, such as little bundles of tobacco. The wands were left at altars, upright with the offerings fastened near the top. The Mesquakies used the root bark to cure canker sores, and the Cheyenne used the fruit mixed with salt to alleviate soreness of the mouth. White settlers made a tea of the bark and sweetened it with sugar and honey as a remedy for asthma.

The color of the fruit when ripe is sometimes red, sometimes reddish orange, and sometimes the same warm red-into-violet that the thickets turn in midwinter, as if each frozen branch were a long tube storing up color for summer. To the glassy blue of a winter sky, to the black fields, to the smoky gray-brown stands of trees along the creeks, to the white scraps of snowdrifts lying in the furrows, to the gold of grasses and weeds, the plum thickets add their own primary color, a deep burgundy like nothing else on the plains. You could squeeze out only those six hues on a palette and it would immediately look like winter in Nebraska.

Unfortunately, the road maintenance crews don't like plum thickets. They contend that the bushes cause snow to drift onto the roads, and in a number of counties, there is a routine of spraying the plums with herbicides. My home territory, Seward County, persists in this idiocy, which makes the road crews feel better but does little good against the snowdrifts, since the dead thicket remains to catch the wind just as if it were alive. I once asked a county official why these crews didn't just cut the thickets down, and he said, "Our men are too old to be climbing up and down in those ditches."

But the plums, thriving on the red sap of their wildness, survive even the government. Plums are too wild for their herbicides, for their Roundup and Tordon and 24D, too wild for their sour spit and their curses, for the subzero Januaries, the grass fires of spring, the kilnlike days of mid-August. Wild Plum, wild *Prunus americana*, member of the rose family, more fragrant than roses. *Prunus* from *prounos*, an ancient

16

Greek name for the plum. And the heady perfume of the wild plum in blossom, drifting through an open window to braid itself softly about us, all wildness itself – how it carries us back even further, to a time before history, to a place through which we grope our way, longing for something we cannot quite define, waving a peeled and painted wand with a packet of tobacco tied to its end. Oh, dear fragrance on the swollen river of spring, sweet wistfulness turning and turning on the speeding black current.

Mid-May, and all afternoon the goldfinches have been harvesting black dandelion seed, flitting from white puff to white puff, burning those little black pellets of coal. Last winter, they were all in khaki, wearing their army surplus overcoats. But inside each of them, through the winter months, one of last summer's dandelion seeds was slowly coming to life, and each breast was beginning to bloom like a bright yellow flower.

Hubert sits in a webbed lawn chair next to his house and asks me, "Did you ever want a cigarette so bad you could kill for it?"

I quit smoking thirty years ago, but I say, "Yes."

"The other day," he says, taking in a deep breath to launch his story, "I was out on the lake in my rowboat, and I got a hankering for a smoke. I had cigarettes, but hard as I looked, I couldn't find a match. I looked all over the boat, in my tackle box, must've went through my pockets five times.

"So I paddled to shore and started looking through my pickup. No matches. I looked under the seat and all. Then I got this idea.

"I was wearing one of them down vests, you know? And I got out my pocketknife and made a little cut inside where it wouldn't show. I pulled out a pinch of that down and laid it on the fender. Then I opened the hood, got out my tools, and took the top off the carburetor float bowl. Then I dipped that pinch of down in the gas and set it on the fender again and quick put the carburetor back together.

"Then I got in and started the engine and jumped out and pulled off one of the spark plug wires just far enough that it would arc across. Then I held that piece of down in the arc, and sure enough it lit. Then I lit that cigarette and sat on the running board and smoked it."

17

Hubert is a make-do sort of fellow, and there are a lot of men like him in rural Nebraska. You learn when you live in the country that you never want to throw away anything that might ever have a possible use. You carry extra books of matches. You keep sheds full of buckets of bent nails and jars of odd screws and bolts because you never know when you might be looking for a nail to straighten.

Among the things I brought back to Nebraska when my sister and I cleared out my mother's house in Iowa were some very old tin cans of spices. I liked the looks of them and put them on a shelf in the basement, thinking, like everybody else in the country, that I might find a use for them one day. Yesterday Kathleen offered to bake a pumpkin pie for me – I love pumpkin pies – but she couldn't find any ground cloves in our spice drawer. I went to the basement, brought up Mother's ancient Schilling's can of cloves, and the pie was marvelous, the best I'd ever tasted. The red-and-gold label on the can was copyrighted in 1933, but that was before Mother and Father set up housekeeping, so it probably didn't date back quite that far. And a company doesn't change the look of its labels very often. But I figure this can was bought at least forty or fifty years ago. Mother didn't use cloves very often, and a can would have lasted a long time. Prying up the rusty lid was like opening King Tut's tomb. There, preserved for the ages, was the spicy fragrance of cloves, as if it had been put there yesterday. How pleased Mother would be that we found a use for it. She was never one to let things go to waste.

At one corner of an abandoned farmhouse stands an ancient lilac bush, a twelve-foot-high splash of rough gray canes rich with a persistent and indomitable green life. Its base, as broad as the trunk of a one-hundred-year-old tree, is a tangle of twisted, cordy wood matted with dead leaves and interwoven through and through by impetuous little runners. Its bushy crest, covered with fragrant blossoms, is like a small violet cloud tethered to the corner of the old house, and it calls into its cool shade a big circle of grass, fallen clapboards, and caving foundation stones.

Like that one great aunt in every family who takes it upon herself to remember the birthdays of every member, this old lilac has set about to chronicle the history of this farmstead. In its withered arms, it has gath-

18

ered the memorabilia of many years. Here is a scrap of white twine, here a corn shuck blown in from a field. In the leaves at its base are a child's tin doll cup and saucer, once blue and white but now dirty with rust. Gathered about the bush are three spark plugs, a broken water glass, and a small piece of oilcloth printed with clusters of cherries. Here is a gear from a forgotten machine; here, two broken robin eggs and a blue milk of magnesia bottle; here, bits of cellophane, a rubber ring from a Mason jar, shreds of tinfoil, pieces of wallpaper printed with pine cones.

And these are merely the items that the bush has decided to keep. Over the years a good many other things have blown up against these stringy branches and then blown on – newspapers, letters from relatives, the weight ticket from the grain scale at the elevator, an auction bill – things lifted on the wind and blown on, over the fence, over the long grass of the pasture, over the brush and willows lining the creek, and out onto the slow brown stream where they settled like leaves and drifted away.

This lilac bush is the figurehead of the ship of this old farm. It breaks the waves of the years, leading the rest of this farmstead into the future, the reluctant faded buildings washing along toward certain destruction, the wind keening in the rigging of the cedars.

I sit this evening in the shade of the lilac, sorting through the curios of this lilac museum and looking off across the shimmering distance toward a distant farmstead with a red barn rising above a dense windbreak of cedars. Perhaps behind those trees is a new white house, a young lilac bush in bloom at one corner, with only a blossom or two on its springy young canes. A young man has just now come in from disking his fields, and he stops to look with pride at his house, his wife's vegetable garden, and his lilac, held upright by a piece of white twine tied to a lath. He stoops to pick a scrap of paper blown in among the canes.

I've been told that one of the reasons you can't make a well-behaved pet out of a wolf is because they are extremely sensitive to the slightest changes in their environment. They stay wild. The Bohemians say, "You may christen a wolf, and he will ask, 'Which way to the wood?'"

People who've tried to tame wolves have learned the animals will im-

19

mediately go on the defensive if the smallest item in a room has been moved. Shifting an ashtray from one table to another is enough to upset them.

Spring
Summer
Autumn
Winter

A plump, soft-bodied, nearly hairless creature like me can't claim much of anything in common with wolves, but since moving to the country, I find I've developed a little of the wolf's attention to change. I lived in the city for many years, where nobody pays any attention to what has been moved from one place to another. In fact, in the city, more things are moving about than are staying in place. A red Buick stopped in front of the house is gone the next instant, replaced by a yellow mini-van; somebody drops a dime by a parking meter, and somebody else comes along and picks it up; nobody thinks much about fresh trash on the sidewalk – a candy wrapper, a dead pigeon, an empty wine bottle. These items will be gone by the next morning, carried away by constant change.

In the country, though, change is customarily as gradual and predictable as the leafing of trees. Because of this, a woman who drives the same few miles of gravel every morning and evening, or a man who every afternoon pauses at the kitchen window to look out across the garden, immediately notices the slightest deviation from the expected. An empty pack of cigarettes lying in the grass fifty yards off will call attention to itself. If during the night a branch has broken from a tree and fallen onto a distant hillside, it will seem as prominent as a flying saucer. If a passerby stops his car to look at a flock of sheep, it is only a matter of seconds before the sheep's owner, rebuilding a lawnmower engine in the open doorway of a barn a quarter of a mile away, has noticed the stranger is there.

And with some of the wolf's defensiveness, people in the country can come to believe that any change occurring at a rate more accelerated than the unfolding of the seasons must be viewed with skepticism. What good can possibly come from that stranger leaning on the fence by the sheep pen?

On the other hand, you can put just about anything over on a small community if you go about it so slowly that you do not alert the wolf in the people who live there. Want to dump some hazardous chemicals in the local landfill? Just bring it a bucket at a time, casually, as if you were carrying water to the chickens. Want to dam up a river? String out the process for so many years that the debate itself becomes a kind of stability. Want to shut down a local school in favor of busing the students to a central place? Just do it a grade at a time.

Our consolidated school district, centered in our county seat, Seward, was successful in slowly closing down services in the schools of the small outlying communities like Garland. The board, recognizing the natural wolf sight of rural people, drew out the pace of this dismemberment for so long that most of the parents in the little towns grew accustomed to the process. The school officials lopped off a few grades at a time, starting with the high school, then the junior high, then sixth grade, then fifth, and so on, not every year, but every few years. It became a matter of course. The students who lost their classrooms were picked up and bused to the big town. The process of attrition reduced the enrollment in the outlying schools, and the school board then noted with mock surprise that, because of decreased enrollment, more of the local schools' services should be cut back. One of my neighbors who still has good wolf sight observed that this was like having the school board members hold open the gate to the corral while they remarked upon how many of the horses were getting away. And so it went, just a bucket or two of this hazardous waste at a time. Sure, there was a shock of disappointment whenever another grade got shorn away, but the parents were so worn down by the inexorable patience of the board that most of them gave up. The wolf in them got old, and its teeth fell out. Its eyes grew clouded by cataracts from having watched this process go on for so many years. What the school board considered progress – consolidation – was to others the death of a valuable institution, the village school. But at the final meeting with the school board, only a handful of parents showed up. Those few people who attended were still alert enough to notice that the ashtray had finally been moved from one table to another.

The gradual incursion of rural housing developments is as insidious as the closing of a local school. A person with wolf sight can spot a splash of fluorescent orange paint on a surveyor's stake a quarter mile off. The hills where I live are about twenty miles from the edge of the capital city, close enough to permit commuting and far enough away to hold the promise of a peaceful life in the country. The majority of our county commissioners thinks that housing developments are good for the county, despite the objections of the people who live there and the cost of providing the services that new residents demand: improved roads, fire and ambulance service, and buses to deliver children to the consolidated school. This majority of commissioners, described as "yeasty" by one of my witty neighbors, is puffed up on the illusory promise of new tax revenue and has been slowly nibbling away at our comprehensive plan to permit residential development wherever a developer might want to put it.

One recently approved residential development in our area was vigorously opposed by the county planning and zoning commission, local landowners, and the state Game and Parks Commission, but it was approved. The opponents of the development testified that neighboring agricultural land prices would be inflated, farming practices such as aerial spraying would be interfered with, and the area available for hunting and fishing would be compromised. They noted the scarcity of reliable water in the area and a soil quality so poor that septic systems might not properly percolate. Concerns were expressed about runoff into the lake. But the commissioners approved it anyway, holding the interests of the developer above those of the people who live in the area.

So, little by little, the countryside shows more and more signs of change, and the wolves among us grow more and more uneasy. The orange stakes go up on the hillsides, followed by white PVC pipes marking new wells. Then a new gravel lane appears, turning away into a field; then a backhoe appears by a new gate, waiting to dig a foundation. We who are concerned about the possible effects of these isolated residential developments on our traditions and our county infrastructure, we who attend public hearings and voice our objections, we know all the while that the people are at this moment powerless against county officials who have befriended the developers despite the opposition of the people. As the Bohemians say, "Money is a master everywhere."

Alice doesn't like to get wet, but our little black-and-white polka-dot pointer, Hattie, who died this year at sixteen, loved to catch frogs. She'd

22

spend an entire day intently nosing along through the deep grass at the edge of the pond, quivering with excitement. When she sniffed out a frog, she'd go on point, her tail straight as a stick, and then she'd pounce.

Sometimes she'd nab one by the back feet in midjump and prance along holding it high, swinging it like a fat sack of nickels, its long legs desperately flexing to get free, its little hands squeezing the empty air. I won't get into what she'd do with it later.

Early in the spring, when the frogs were beginning to emerge from their winter beds deep in the bank of the pond, Hattie could be found splashing along the edge, excitedly sniffing for breathing holes. When she smelled what she was looking for, she'd try to dig it out, barking and barking, her forefeet churning up a plume of muddy water.

That's where Buddy came in. He's a formidable foe for a frog, with a head like an anvil and jaws like an alligator. Setting off his big head is a soft muzzle of deep pink that makes him look as if he's just been eating raspberries.

Whenever it would dawn on Buddy that Hattie was getting too much attention from one of us, he'd shoulder her out of the way, and during the years since he'd strayed onto our place during the night and moved right into her doghouse, she'd gotten used to his selfish behavior. She'd also grown wiser with age, and she'd turned that pushiness of his to her own use when it came to frog hunting. She was an older dog, you must remember, with a little sprinkle of silver on her muzzle and a little stiffness in the joints. She was still quick, but she preferred to save her quickness until she really needed it.

She'd start to dig out a frog, barking and whimpering as she pawed the bank, knowing that Buddy couldn't stand it that she seemed to be having so much fun. He'd come galloping from wherever he was, his huge feet thudding over the ground, ears flapping. At full speed, he'd throw a body block into her and set to doing the digging himself, his big shoulder muscles rolling under his skin. He dug more slowly than she did, but his was serious, earth-moving, dog-wearying digging, and he could excavate an enormous yawning hole in just a few minutes, covering himself with mud in the process.

Hattie would stand back, barking excitedly, urging him on, getting

23

him to do the hard work. Now and then she'd rush in to keep him inspired and then jump back when he turned to growl at her. Then, when he at last uncovered the blinking, hapless frog, she'd dash in, snap up the prize, and run off with it, leaving Buddy squinting through muddy brows into the empty pit he'd dug. Once she worked him so hard that he tore loose one of the claws on his right forepaw, and we had to take him to the vet to have it pulled off with pliers. Hattie went along just for the ride, letting him sit up front in the wind while she sat in the back seat and gazed out the window.

Because my son, Jeff, would soon graduate from college and move many miles away, I'd gotten very busy with my hands. The orderly world of our lives together was spinning out of control, and I spent nearly all of my free time fixing, straightening, sorting, and resorting. Losing someone you love can make you want to count every nail and bolt and washer you own. "He who has daughters has a family," the Bohemians say, "and he who has sons has strangers."

My first wife and I were divorced when Jeff was two, and he'd grown up with her in Iowa, visiting me in the summers and on holidays. Then he came to Nebraska to finish college, and he'd been living with Kathleen and me for three years. It had been the best time of our lives, having him near.

During that time, he'd set about making the farm his own. He'd fixed up a little apartment in an old corncrib and had even put a washtub on the rafters so that he could drain water into a makeshift sink. He spent most of his time there, his music thudding against the walls, his computer humming. Hattie left Kathleen and me and decided to sleep with him.

He had organized the innards of the garage and the workshop in the barn in his own fashion, putting the tools where he could find them, nailing up makeshift shelves here and there, sorting the cans of nails by size. Soon he knew where everything was, and I didn't know where anything was, but I didn't resent it. It had been my chance to be a full-time father.

Now, in my anguish over his going away, I was beginning to make

24

things worse for both of us by starting to disassemble his order to reimpose my own.

One chilly Saturday while he was in Iowa visiting his girlfriend, I *Spring* sized up his old treehouse. He and a friend had built it one summer – a *Summer* crazy, catawampus collection of old boards, window screens, and ply- *Autumn* wood slung between a clump of three old ash trees. The summer they'd *Winter* built it, they had slept out there for weeks. It was their place on our place, and it had become for me a central symbol of Jeff's place in my life and of all the happiness we'd shared. Now I wanted to tear it to splinters. I wanted to pull it apart and stack up the boards in neat piles and put the nails back in their jar.

Knowing he'd be hurt if I touched his treehouse, I rerouted my energy and dug into a big pile of used bricks that the former owner of our farm had left behind. It was a job that I had asked my son to do several times and that he had started and left unfinished. Now I was going to do it myself. I wouldn't mention it, of course, but he'd see that I'd had to do it myself and be sorry.

The wild plum bushes were in flower. If you stood close enough to take in their perfume, you could hear the bees at work. And I worked like a bee at a flower, head down in concentration. I neatly stacked the good bricks and then loaded up my old pickup with the broken ones and threw them one by one – threw them hard – into a washed-out place on our grassland to the west. That took all morning, a few hours from the short time before my son would be leaving us for good.

The treehouse was still there when I drove back down the drive. It floated above the property, gray as a storm cloud, radiating sentiment. I walked over and stood in its shadow.

The boys had done a good job of building it, fitting the scrap boards together, nailing on roofing material to keep it dry, but it was not so well built that one crazed father with a crowbar couldn't tear it all down in a weekend, leaving no trace. I still held back.

A breeze had come up during the morning, and the trees tugged at the boards, making the joints cry out. Stealthily, I climbed the steps that had been nailed onto one of the supporting trees and peered inside. The space was empty except for a few cow bones in one corner that the boys

25

had found and put there years before. I crawled inside and lay down on the floor, looking up at the roof. This was the way in which the two boys had seen the world. They had lain here and looked up as the nights darkened and the coyotes barked and the oppressive parents slept in their bed in the house. This was how it had felt to be Jeff, once, long ago, when he was a boy. I closed my eyes and listened to the creaking boards and the breezes whistling softly in the branches. I felt the treehouse move just slightly as the wind pushed the trees one way and then another.

Today, the treehouse still floats in the arms of its tree. Some of the roof has pulled open, and rain will eventually rot out the floor. The steps going up the trunk are loose, and I have to warn visiting children to be careful climbing up. I hear them up there talking excitedly about those mysterious cow bones, wondering who might have hidden them there.

The other day, I was in the wooded draw west of my chicken coop cutting up a couple of fallen trees with my chainsaw when one of our neighbors stopped by. He left his wife in his old pickup and came over to talk to me. In our part of the world, women spend a lot of their time waiting in pickups. I killed the engine of the saw and set it down, and we stood and talked. My dogs came over and sniffed the saw and then stretched out nearby to listen in.

This neighbor is a good-looking, happy-go-lucky Czech in his mid-forties. He runs a few cows and calves, does a little of this and a little of that, and raises hunting dogs on the side. He was thinking about building some new portable dog kennels and wanted to ask me what I thought of the idea. I'm a pretty good shade tree carpenter and have built several small buildings on our place.

He described the kennels. He said they'd have a doghouse at one end, opening into a four-foot-by-eight-foot pen. They would be set several feet off the ground. There would be heavy wire screen on the floors of the pens, so the dog droppings would fall through, and he could drag the kennels around his pasture on wooden skids to keep the manure from piling up in one place. I told him they sounded like big rabbit hutches, and he said that sounded about right.

He got to talking about putting a one-by-six here and a two-by-six there, and I told him I couldn't quite follow. "Here's what I mean," he said. There was an old board lying nearby, and he got down on his knees and scratched a drawing on the board with a pair of pliers he had pulled out of his coveralls. It took him ten seconds. "See?" he said. I saw, immediately.

Spring

Summer

Autumn

Winter

After he left, I got to thinking about the act of drawing and how complicated it's gotten. In my house, about a hundred feet from where we'd been talking, I have a computer with a program that you can use to make drawings. The computer cost quite a lot and so did the drawing program. The drawing program doesn't do anything that a fellow can't do with a pair of pliers and an old board, and it isn't any faster. In fact, it's a good deal slower. The act of making a computer drawing is once removed from real drawing. A step is added. You have to know how to draw, first, and then how to make the computer draw for you. It's like writing a draft of a letter in a foreign language and then translating it back into English.

If I'd set out to draw that same dog kennel on the computer, it would've taken me ten minutes. But my neighbor did it on an old board in ten seconds.

This has reminded me of my favorite example of technology on the march. A mail carrier friend told me this one. A few years ago, the main post office in Lincoln got authorization to buy a fancy new letter-sorting machine. In order to justify the expense – many thousands of dollars – the machine had to process a certain number of letters each day. Well, in Lincoln, they didn't have nearly enough letters coming through to justify the expense of the machine. So what did they do? They wanted that machine so much that they sorted the mail through once, and then they sorted it again.

A lot of people complain about not having enough time to do what they really want to do. In an age when technological advances have supposedly reduced the need for manual labor, there ought to be a lot more leisure time for all of us. But there isn't, everybody seems to agree. The fact is, computers are eating some of our time. All over the country, right now, people are sitting transfixed at their screens, using their computers to do things that could be done a lot faster with a pencil and paper.

We have an outdoor toilet. I've learned to follow that announcement with the assurance that we have indoor plumbing too, just so people won't get the idea that we're "funny." But I suspect the locals think we are funny, outdoor toilet or not. Nobody in Nebraska is all that much at ease with a writer in the neighborhood.

All of our neighbors have torn down their outhouses and have filled the holes with beer bottles and rubble and have planted hollyhocks over the site. Most of them wouldn't hesitate for an instant before relieving themselves off the side porch, but it's considered to be backward to have an outdoor toilet that "still works."

Where we live, real estate isn't considered modern if you own an outdoor toilet. In our area, the term *modern* always means indoor plumbing. That's what the motel signs mean when they say "modern rooms." And when they say "clean modern rooms," that tells you they pay somebody to clean the toilets.

We call ours an outdoor toilet, but as you know, they have at least a dozen names: outhouse, backhouse, privy, johnny, and so on. I don't know why it's necessary to have so many different names, but I suppose it's natural to be a little ambivalent about a place like that. Each of us comes at an outdoor toilet from a slightly different perspective.

Ours is an old one, built seventy or eighty years ago, judging from the age of our other farm buildings. All of our buildings are well built, the bequests of a good country carpenter, and the outdoor toilet is square and plumb, made of full-dimension yellow pine two-by-fours and neatly joined cedar clapboards. You can peer into the open grain of the siding and see that the building has always been red. It's a one-hole, two-hook toilet. You can hook the door from the inside or the outside, depending upon which way you're headed, in or out.

Some outdoor toilets are two-holers, as you probably know. An acquaintance of mine bought an old farm from an elderly woman who had moved to a neighboring town. Whenever she had a question about the farm, she'd call the old woman, who always seemed happy to oblige her with an answer. One day she called and asked, "I've noticed that the two holes in the outdoor toilet are of different sizes, one little one and one bigger one. Was that for children and adults?" "No, honey," the woman replied, "winter and summer."

Unlike the outhouses on comic postcards from the Ozarks, ours doesn't have a little moon cut into the door, so you need to leave the door ajar or you'll find yourself in the dark with spiders and wasps and maybe a curious mouse. When you're in our outdoor toilet, or any of them for that matter, your bare bottom is perched right on the edge of the natural world. This can be unsettling for people accustomed to modern facilities. In the summer, you have to warn visitors about black widow spiders who build webs just under the seat and attack whatever might be hanging there. I always advise our guests it's best to take a little toilet paper and take a quick swipe around the underside of the seat. That'll knock the spiders loose. Mud dauber wasps build their nests up against the rafters but they're not likely to sting you unless you aggravate them.

The other day I noticed some small animal had burrowed under one side of the building, letting a beam of light down into the pit. God knows why it would want to sit and read down there, but there's no accounting for taste. I haven't told any of our visitors that there might be some little creature down there looking up with wonder at their bottoms.

Our outdoor toilet doesn't get much use in winter, and the mice take it over as soon as the snow flies. By spring the seat and floor are littered with broken acorn hulls. One of my first spring chores is to sweep these away. I'm fond of mice and admire their tireless industry, and I like to think of them scampering around in there in the dark while blinding white blizzards rage beyond the door. Because the mice like to tear up the toilet paper for their nests, I keep a roll in a two-gallon stone crock with a yellow dinner plate on top. So far it's got them baffled, but it seems to baffle our guests too. They don't think to look in there for the paper unless you tell them about it.

We moved our outdoor toilet to where it now sits. When we were getting ready to make an offer to purchase the place, we sized up all the buildings. In the shadowy outdoor toilet, we took a sly look down through the hole in the seat and discovered that the pit had been filled to the top with broken bricks, blue milk of magnesia bottles, and miscellaneous farm trash, including a white porcelain doorknob that glowed in the shadows like a mysterious egg. With a full pit, the building wasn't

29

of much use, and, besides, it was much too close to the house and the well.

Spring
Summer
Autumn
Winter

Some months after the property was ours, my son and I spent the better part of a week digging a new pit east of the barn. I'd never dug a big businesslike hole like that and felt like an archeologist as we spaded down through layers of antique feedlot mud and gooey yellow clay. We found an old harness buckle and the rusty traces of other mysterious metal pieces long since absorbed by the earth. From time to time, the two of us sat on the bottom and rested. It was cool and damp, and the broad Nebraska sky was reduced to a blue rectangle across which an occasional barn swallow darted. My son lit a cigarette, and the smoke pooled like water in a well. Our dogs came to the edge and peered down at us, feeling diminished by creatures who could dig a hole that big.

When we got the hole as deep and square as we wanted it, we put a piece of plywood over the top to keep trespassers from stumbling in. We knew it would be a while before we got up the initiative to move the building. It was the kind of project you want to think about for a long time. One day my wife and a little boy climbed down in the hole during a hide-and-seek game, having found the most improbable hiding place on the farm. The little boy's older sister stood on the sheet of plywood and shrieked with rage, flummoxed by the voices calling out to her in a whisper from the earth at her feet.

While we were thinking about how to move it, I put in a new plywood floor, built a new one-holer bench, installed a new oak toilet seat with a hinged lid, plugged up a few cracks that let the wasps in under the eaves, and put on a fresh coat of red paint. It was ready to go on the road.

One Sunday afternoon we chained the pickup to it and dragged it over to the hole. It was a slow and comic processional of about seventy-five yards, across the lane and around behind the barn, the little building wobbling crazily on its skids, the fan belt of the old pickup screaming and smoking.

It's nicely situated now. It faces the rising sun and overlooks a wooded draw that in the early morning light is drenched with dew, the soft light sparkling in the tiny beads of water on the leaves. Because of the new burrow in the side, there's a cool breeze just under the seat. Just outside

the door are a couple of oak saplings you can watch grow while you sit
there off and on for the next twenty or thirty years.

That's looking out from inside. From the other direction, as you ap-
proach our place along the gravel road, you see the outdoor toilet standing alone against the trees in the distance, its door hooked, maybe somebody in there, maybe not, the little building not looking majestic by any
means but looking as if it ought to be right where it is. Looking a little
"funny" too, I suppose.

🍂

Spring is the time to order baby chicks from the Murray McMurray
hatchery in Webster City, Iowa, and to wait for Iris to phone one morning from the post office to tell you that the box has arrived, but we're not
ordering any this year. We have a dozen old hens on pension, and I don't
want to start a new batch until these senior citizens have gone to their
reward. Most of my neighbors would have had them stewed with homemade egg noodles by now, but we're too soft hearted to kill them. They
do deliver now and then at a cost, in feed, of about a dollar per egg.

Because I don't like to step into their muddy pen in the morning, I
toss their feed over the fence. I use a tin can for a launcher and throw it
with enough strength that the feed spreads out over the ground as it
falls, giving all the hens a chance at it.

They've gotten conditioned to this routine. When they hear me rattling the lid of the garbage can that holds their food, they fan out
downfield, looking back toward me like football players waiting for a
long pass. "Go long! Go long!" they seem to be clucking.

🍂

Another of my neighbors, who has since moved on, was a furniture de-
signer and wood craftsman who liked to make bowls from Osage orange.
I have one of these beautiful bowls before me, as yellow as the inside of
an acorn squash and heavy and hard as alabaster. It takes a fine, high
polish and has a remarkable, mysterious feeling to it, as if it might be
radioactive. Just holding it you feel as if you are clinging to something
flying through the universe at the speed of light.

This neighbor happened to be the son of a craftsman of a different
kind of permanence, a five-star Air Force general who had been com-

31

mander of the Skylab project, commander in chief of NORAD, and vice chairman of the Joint Chiefs of Staff. His craft was war. While, outside Garland, my neighbor removed his work from his turning lathe and weighed it in his talented hands, his father sat at a desk in the Pentagon, holding the fate of the world.

Spring
Summer
Autumn
Winter

Osage orange is a wood with a long history. Prized by the Indians for their bows, and named by the French trappers *Bois d'Arc*, it was later planted by the settlers of the Great Plains as a hedge used to pen in livestock before the introduction of barbed wire. Osage hedges were said to be "pig tight." During the past 125 years, these hedges have grown up into twenty- and thirty-foot trees. By dropping their bright green orangelike fruit, commonly called hedge apples, they sire successive generations. To this day, thick twisted borders of Osage are a common sight on the prairies.

For a long time farmers have used Osage for fence posts because it is almost as strong and durable as steel and free for the cutting. It's said an Osage post will outlast the posthole, and it's not uncommon for them to last fifty years, exposed to the rot-inducing wet-then-dry weather of the Great Plains. Given the reputation of Osage orange, my neighbor's beautiful bowls, given an occasional dusting and kept on a table inside, ought to last almost forever. At the least, they ought to have a thousand-year half-life, like some of the things made under the supervision of his father. Sometimes I dream of those golden bowls flying out beyond the farthest planet and into deep space, like the Voyager II, carrying their indecipherable message into the future.

The general and his son were dark-haired, dark-eyed, handsome, likeable men. I met the general for the first time about fifteen years ago, at his son's wedding. He and I stood in the smoke and red glow of the barbeque grill and overcooked a chicken together. Earlier that same week, I'd spent an evening with the Russian poet Yevgeny Yevtushenko, and as I stood barbequing with the general, who at that time held the grand title (believe me!) of commander of space, I wondered in silence what had brought me to this peculiar intersection of east and west.

I saw the general again just as the first revelations of the Iran-Contra affair were making it into the newspapers. The general and his wife were back in Nebraska to visit their grandchildren. He was out in my neighbor's woodworking shop, tapping with hammer and chisel, smoothing an upright post. Trying to make conversation, I suggested that he was probably happy to be working with his hands in Nebraska instead of answering questions in Washington. He responded with a friendly but weary smile, then turned back to his task and ran his fingers over the raw wood with its simple, straightforward, altogether predictable grain.

Spring
Summer
Autumn
Winter

Lots of Avon: For those of you who like to go out now and then to see live theater, yet who live in communities where there is no local players' group and where the school plays are few and far between, I enthusiastically recommend neighborhood garage sales. They're inexpensive (little more than the price of a gallon of gas) and you don't have to stand around at intermission sipping white wine and nibbling goat cheese and trying to sound as if you know something about art. And just as when watching a play, you have the opportunity to poke around in other people's business while discreetly standing off at a safe distance.

Those of us who love garage sales begin watching the classified ads in early spring. The first sales of the year, with people hunched up in overcoats and gloves, crowding garages smelling of antifreeze, are one of life's great pleasures.

Have you ever noticed how much a garage is like a theater? And how much the people having garage sales are like actors placed here and there on a stage? Is it merely a coincidence that Avon bottles are prominently featured in the newspaper advertisements ("LOTS OF AVON") when Shakespeare lived and worked at Stratford-on-Avon? It's a literary allusion! The parallels go on and on.

Let's take a quick look at a typical Saturday matinee at an off-off-off-Broadway garage sale. You enter the cool shade of the theatre and study the set.

For a curtain, we have, of course, the garage door. At some sales, the audience must wait out front until the door is raised (most garage sale devotees resent this). At most sales, though, the curtain is already up by the time you walk past the parked bicycles and down the wide aisle of the driveway.

33

For a backdrop (in the theatre it would be the "cyclorama"), there is a shadowy rear wall hung with bent rakes and snarled Weed Eaters marked NOT FOR SALE. Or maybe everything back there in the darkness is draped with a pink chenille bedspread with torn fringe. This adds a little suspense. It's anyone's guess what may be behind it and how whatever it is will fit into the action.

Remember your stage directions? Downstage is toward the front, upstage is toward the back. Right and Left are to the right and left of the actors. The set includes – along with lots of tables heaped with rummage – an old card table downstage right. It's prominently lit because it protrudes just a little way out into the sunlight. It's a brown cardboard table, scuffed white on the corners from being slid in and out of a closet for years. At the table are two folding chairs.

There are two actors at the table, a leggy woman in her thirties and a little girl. The woman has a long thin cigarette dangling from her lips. The ash is about to fall into her lap. Her coppery hair is tightly wrapped around pink rollers, and her head looks as if it were entirely covered with coils from an electric motor. The little girl is taking change out of a cigar box and counting it into neat little stacks and licking her fingertips to taste the sourness. Now and then, the woman reaches over and pulls the girl's hand away from her mouth. These actors are aware of their audience, but they scarcely acknowledge that you are there.

From a screen door at stage right, ENTER AN OLD WOMAN. She is wearing an apron and carrying a soft, leaky puppy at arm's length. She turns to the audience and says, "Can't use a good dog can you?"

LITTLE GIRL, upset: "Grandma! That's Misty's puppy!"

And so on . . . the drama unfolds.

There are a number of standard comedies, many of them featuring a debate between family members over the personal history of some prop, as in, "It's real old. Aunt Violet gave it to the folks for a wedding present."

"No, Ginger. You're dead wrong about that."

As you can see, most of the playwrights use local dialects and idioms. Listening to the actors talk is one of the great pleasures of attending these sales. Where I live, one common usage is diff'rent. As when enumer-

34

ating the virtues of an amateur oil painting by an absent family member: "That's sure diff'rent," or "That painting of Jill's, it's real diff'rent, that's for sure."

If you like tragedy, you can find a melancholy edge to many of these little side street dramas: the beautiful handwork of some lost grandmother, every stitch marking off a minute stolen from a hard life, the faces in family photographs bought for their frames, the dried-out shoes of some old man. "All life is but a passing shadow . . ." There's a little sadness at the edge of every sale, the sorrow of some gift once cherished stuffed into a cardboard box with the one-legged doll and the dominoes.

And there's a little sex, of course. There's something vaguely arousing about being in a space stacked high with intimate personal disclosures, each carrying the intoxicating fragrance of strangeness. By looking around, you can learn almost more than you want to know about that young woman. "We are such stuff as dreams are made on."

And so on. You get the point. That's our Saturday matinee. "Our revels now have ended." You may recall the old high school standard *You Can't Take it With You*, by Moss Hart and George S. Kaufman. It's one of many popular plays about a family crisis that gets resolved happily. Every school in America has performed it dozens of times. In ways, its tone is so much like a family holding a garage sale that you have to wonder if the authors weren't thinking of one. But at a garage sale, you *can* take it with you. At the end of the play, when these weary actors get ready to draw down the wooden curtain, they may even *give* you the props.

"You take a dime for that?"

The auction season is also starting up, and I went to a sale the other day. The school district was selling fixtures and equipment from several of the small village schools that it has closed. There were a lot of people there who had gone to those schools and who wanted to bid on the desks, some of which still had their initials carved into them. I bought an antique opaque projector, with a lens the size of a car headlight, that I can use in painting signs. You're welcome in a small community if there's something you can do, and I can paint signs.

While I stood at the back of the crowd, I got into a conversation with a

35

man I've seen around, about fifty, tall, with mutton chop sideburns. I don't know how we got to the subject of deer – perhaps he steered us in that direction – but he told me about a blind doe that has been coming around his cabin on the Blue River south and west of the alps. It comes to his garden fence and touches the top wire with its nose as if to place it, then jumps over and feeds on his young lettuce and spinach till he goes out and shouts it away. He said the doe can remember just where the fence wire was and clears it with ease and runs down into the trees by the river, bumping into them as it goes. I haven't been able to get this out of my mind. How long could a blind deer possibly live?

I just counted twenty-seven turkey vultures perched in the trees at the head of our pond, taking the early morning sun, a few holding their wings open as if to air them like soiled bedding after a long winter, others lazily shifting from branch to branch, their weight slightly altering the white shapes of the dead trees as they settle. Gray-brown feathers like ash, little red heads like lumps of innards. If we were looking for one word to describe them, it would be patience. The turkey vulture is never in a hurry; what it wants will come to it in time.

Two years ago in late spring, when Kathleen drove me home from the hospital after my cancer surgery, we came up over a hill about a mile from our house, and they were waiting, maybe fifty turkey vultures, sitting on fence posts along the road, standing in the grass just over the fence. Uh-oh, I thought, they've been waiting for me. I might as well get out and lie down at the edge of the road.

As they moved about on the ground, they occasionally opened and then beat down their wings, lifting them just slightly off the ground, as if to say, I can fly if I feel like it, but I don't feel like it just yet. There will be plenty time for flying later. For the time being, we're waiting. Just working our wings a little and slowly turning our heads and showing off the red fists of our heads and our bright yellow eyes that can see right straight through human hope.

Summer

*Only a pumpkin is a head
without cares.*

Maybe not in the Bohemian Alps, but somewhere in rural Nebraska, along a gravel road, comes what could be the Fourth of July parade float for this year's Poison Queen. It's a red-and-white '78 Ford pickup, creeping along at maybe five miles an hour, fenders rattling and muffler popping. One of the rearview mirrors swings from its bolt like a saucepan. There's an air compressor and a big white plastic tank in the back, sloshing with a milky fluid. All this is followed by a rising plume of yellow dust, the sweet perfume of leaking brake fluid, and the peculiar metallic odor of herbicide. The conveyances in which Death comes riding arrive in all manner of guises.

One man stands in the back, next to the tank, and another is in the cab, one elbow out in the wind like the snout of a torpedo. Strips of duct tape hold the windshield together, and the driver peers out between them. Let's guess, there's a cooler full of iced-down beer on the passenger's seat, and the crotch of the driver's overalls is soaked from squeezing a can between his thighs.

The man in the back does the spraying. To keep his belly counterbalanced, he presses his hams back against the chemical tank while he swivels back and forth and bathes the ditch with herbicide. Below the sleeves of his T-shirt, his fat arms glisten with sweat and poison. There's a gleam in his eyes as he peers out from under the bill of his cap, cigarette clenched in his teeth: Rambo wielding a flamethrower.

Behind the rolling truck, the herbicide beads up on the grasses, trickles down the troughs of the blades, and runs into cracks in the soil. Crickets gleam under the wet lacquer of poison, and field mice, huddled in nests in old beer cans, lick the moisture from the fur of their little ones. In a week to ten days, the leaves on all of these plants will turn a dried-blood brown, a color like nothing else in summer.

A good part of the spray lifts and drifts, wafted along on the breeze. You can smell it for a quarter mile. There's a state regulation against spraying when the wind is over six miles an hour, but in Nebraska the wind never blows that softly. Throw your hat up in the air anywhere in these hills and you have to run fast to get to the place where it comes down again.

Spring

Summer

Autumn

Winter

These two aren't official county employees. The county hires them by the hour. Both get most of their income from farming little patches of ground. They're just filling in for a week or so with a little low-speed weed killing at a few dollars an hour. The air compressor and the chemical tank belong to the county, and the poison is the county's too, but the pickup belongs to the driver. One of the doors – the yellow one on the passenger's side – belongs to the man in the back, but that's another story.

If they were county employees, they'd probably be required to wear protective clothing and chemical masks, and they'd have health insurance and disability benefits when their lungs went bad or when their leukocyte count went off the chart. But they don't. If they get sick, they're on their own. And they aren't the kind to sue the county. Farm boys, they grew up victims of the whims of weather and markets, and like so many farmers, they'll go to their graves as victims, believing that Fate ordained that they'd draw the short straws. Few of their neighbors have ever hired a lawyer to prosecute a lawsuit. People in rural communities prefer to settle things themselves, or never to settle them at all, and resentments live through generations.

The county's policy is to kill all the wild plum bushes and sumac and all the miscellaneous little saplings that volunteer in the ditch by the road. They also spray the branches of full-grown trees if their branches hang over the road.

While these two hapless men are killing the things they're paid to be killing, they're spraying nearly everything else as well: the sunflowers, the pink wild roses, the wild grapevines, the chokecherries. If something's living in the ditch, or maybe just over the fence, it's fair game. The weeds set back from the road are the most fun anyway, because you get to screw down the nozzle and spray a lot farther.

Earlier today, they soaked the ditch, the driveway, and the mailbox in front of a widow's house. She's lived there alone since her husband died of cancer, and right now she's probably out in the garden assessing the damage to her roses. Her children are grown and gone. Her husband, a

40

farmer, was of the first generation to use chemicals. He didn't think to worry about the dangers of herbicides and insecticides. When the nozzles on his spraying equipment got plugged up, he put them in his mouth and blew them out. If he got chemicals on his hands, he wiped them on his overalls. When he drained his spray tanks, he did it in the corner of a field.

Most farmers are more careful these days. Those air-conditioned glassed-in cabs on the tractors may look like an expensive luxury, but they keep the chemicals out of the driver's lungs. Most ag workers read and follow the instructions, though at the tavern in Garland I once overheard one of our neighbors say he just mixes different kinds of chemicals together, a little of this and a little of that. He says it doesn't seem to make much difference. They all work, sooner or later. This man never was screwed down real tight, as we say around here.

The chemigators – high-production farmers who mix herbicides and insecticides with the water pumping through center-pivot irrigation systems – generally follow the chemical companies' instructions, but I know of one notable exception. A couple of years ago a farmer in western Nebraska was reported to have thought that mixing the chemicals above ground took too much time. So he poured a barrel of herbicide down the shaft of his irrigation well where it would get all mixed in proper (and mixed into the water table too). The Czechs say, "Do not spit into a well; you do not know when you will drink out of it yourself."

Most of the eight thousand people in our county have the good sense to come in out of the rain and out of the spray. Oh, the people in Garland and Loma and Brainard may stuff a few empty chemical bottles or half-full cans of paint into the bottoms of their garbage bags, thinking the people who run the landfill won't notice, and some farmers still change their oil in the side yard and let the used oil soak into the earth, and the man who delivers the liquid propane sometimes splashes it over his lap, but most people are relatively responsible when it comes to handling and disposing of hazardous chemicals. Let's say that 99.9 percent of Nebraskans aren't dangerous. Part of the other tenth of a percent just drove past with their tank and hose.

❧

About an hour ago, Alice treated herself to a fat mother mouse, and now she's asleep in a patch of sunlight on the porch. She didn't kill and eat it right in front of me but gently closed her jaws around it as if it were a precious roll of nickels and carried it, tail twitching against her muzzle, behind the barn. When she came back, it was gone.

We'd been down by the pond in my "library," a shack where I keep extra books. I was trying to find a reference that would tell me what you are supposed to call the daughter of a second cousin – third cousin or second cousin once removed? While I was leafing through my books, Alice was warning the mouse by loudly snorting into a box of kindling. She announced herself from all four sides before she began to pull out the wood a piece at a time.

The mouse had been spending a pleasant morning in her nest of pee-dampened cotton, part of the stuffing from a hen-shaped pillow I'd left too long on my platform rocker. With her, she had four other mice, children, perhaps, brothers or sisters or nephews and nieces, all spared when she scampered out under the screen door and Alice crashed out after her.

Mice have extended families, no laws against incest, and pay little attention to just how each of them is related to the next. A second cousin once removed is just another mouth to feed. Until some dog removes it. But a human can spend a good hour puzzling: If Connie Dodge was my second cousin, is her daughter Jane my second cousin once removed?

I'd just received a letter from Jane, and with it she'd enclosed a 1915 photograph of her mother, Connie, as an unhappy, sour-faced, four-year-old girl. With Connie in the picture were her curly-haired father, Chelsea Ruth, Chelsea's broad-faced homely mother, Minerva Belle Kooser Ruth, and a woman I'd never before that moment seen, Minerva's tiny, shyly smiling ancient mother, Margaret Elizabeth Boucher Kooser, my great grandmother.

It's a wonderful thing to get your first look at your great grandmother, who died thirty years before you were born. She looks like a lovely person, hands folded in her lap, head tipped to one side, the way I tip my head when I am photographed. As a boy, my father was devoted to her and as a grown man often spoke of her, telling my sister and me that because of obscure, mysterious religious beliefs she wore *not so much as a single button* on her clothes, *only hooks and eyes*. But in this picture her clothes look just like everybody else's, like Minerva's, like Chelsea's. Though the photo is poorly reproduced, I think I can see an ordinary pearl button at the collar of her dress. My father was good at making a good story better.

Spring
Summer
Autumn
Winter

I'm back in the house now, thinking about how much my family means to me. Alice is sprawled on the porch, deep in a full-bellied sleep, and down near our pond, the mouse's relatives have come back from the four dusty corners of my library shack and are gathered next to the silent kindling box, sniffing one another to be sure that each is the mouse that he or she seems to be.

A person needn't be fearful of sixty-five-year-old Mennonite women in white lace caps. They won't come at you waving Bibles. I'm in regular weekly contact with several of them, and they seem to me to be pretty much like most rural women their age. My sample is drawn from behind the counter at the Etcetera Thrift and Gift Shop in Seward, Nebraska, operated by the Mennonite church, and I offer the following observations, made over a period of several years: (1) Mennonite women in their sixties are wary of strangers but grow friendly if approached with friendliness and will gladly search out a sack for your purchases. (2) They handle each article with reverence, as if it had personality and character; they have a winning way of looking upon a homely paint-by-number picture or a tweed sports coat that's a little bit stinky under the arms. You can tell that though they may be glad to see it go, they wish it a happy future. (3) They know the quality of every item in the Lord God's realm and will tell you when the cloudy mirror you've brought to their counter is "a real good bargain too." (4) They customarily work in teams of two, one reading aloud from the price tag and the other scrutinizing the keys on the cash register, then punching each key with stiff-fingered determination, as if an error might send an innocent man to his death. (5) They are extremely careful about counting out change and will do it over and over and over. My mother could have been a Mennonite.

I like these women immensely. They live with goodness and in goodness, and they make it a practical matter. I would like to have them for my kindly, loving aunts, but for the fact that I am about the same age.

Menno Simons, who founded their church in 1537 after leaving the priesthood, recommended a simple life, a simple way of worshipping. My eleventh edition of the *Encyclopedia Britannica* describes his writings as follows: "through them shines a character attractive by the sincerity of its simple and warm spirituality." You can see that character in these women. There's a whole lot worth liking under those little white caps. In smiling pairs they stand behind their scratched wood counter, their hands in the open. And these women at their homely station, with their old cash register full of nickels and dimes, holding your crumpled sack full of secondhand shirts, all these are offered in one package, like a very good bargain from the open hand of God.

In Nebraska, boats travel much farther by land than by water. You see them on highways, back roads, city streets, strapped to trailers and towed by pickups and sports utility vehicles. A boat may go thirty or forty miles to be lowered into the water of a pond not much bigger than a football field. People who live near oceans or the Great Lakes find this peculiar. They aren't used to seeing so many boats on the road. They let theirs rest at moorings or in boat sheds close to the water. But in Nebraska, towing a boat is a kind of informal public relations campaign for the travel and tourism industry. If somebody thinking of moving to our state sees a big boat parked in downtown Lincoln, he or she knows that there really is water somewhere within driving distance.

All morning, pickups towing boats have been rumbling past our place, raising dust, headed for Branched Oak Lake, three miles east. They're driving as fast as they can in order to get their boats into the water before everybody else. Branched Oak Lake is a good-sized body of water for eastern Nebraska, maybe two miles wide and three miles long, room for a lot of boats, but it's fun to be first on the water. Not really big boats, of course. A big boat looks like a toad in a birdbath. Small boats, little speedboats, bass boats with swivel chairs.

44

It's a man-made lake, kept full by rains that run down out of the Bohemian Alps. The dam was built in the 1960s, and it took a long time to fill. A couple of local families owned farms that were in the way of the rising water, and the government condemned their land. An old man told me recently that his aunt, a single woman in old age, refused to leave her house. "She just kept going back there," he said. "They'd come and take her away, and pretty soon she'd be back. Finally, they had to go down there and break all the windows out of the house to get her to leave." The signs read Recreation Area. Her house is underneath it somewhere.

The Bohemian Alps is a worn place in the carpet of grass we know as the Great Plains, the spot where the glaciers wiped their snowy galoshes coming in and out.

Two miles from our house, some of that carpet's cordy backing shows through. It's a limestone quarry, and I like to go over there and sit for a while in the dusty lap of time. There's usually nobody around because the quarry is used only when crushed rock is needed, and stillness pools like rainwater.

I like the exposed layers of rock with their reliable order, thousands of years stacked on shelves like old courthouse ledgers, the oldest on the bottom and the most recent on top, seashells stuck between the pages like bookmarks marking passages in time, an occasional fish pressed flat and black like the tongue of a shoe.

I like the girlish cottonwood saplings, trying to find a life for themselves near the rain pools, persuaded by the slightest wind. I like the iron clutter of labor, the rusty rock-grinding machinery, the bent-up bulldozers baking in the sun, and the broken-down trucks wearing their shattered reading glasses.

The digging there started a long time ago, a couple hundred yards east of the road, and over the years it gradually moved west, following the veins of the most accessible stone. When the hole got up against the gravel road, the county bent the road out and around it. That was at least thirty years ago, a temporary fix that soon became permanent.

45

There've been Road Closed signs there ever since, but the road isn't closed. Or, let's say, the *straight* road is closed, the *curved* road is open. Though it is "temporary," good-sized trees have grown up along it, anchoring it in place.

It's one of the few curving roads in a county where every lane and village sidewalk is laid out on a north-south, east-west grid, so it's a treat to sweep around that curve in your pickup, the centrifugal force pushing you over against your door, your Michelin Wild Country tires throwing up a plume of hundred-thousand-year-old limestone dust.

Engineers prefer things straight. The best road, they think, is the shortest. It was ever so. No farmer would want to take horse and wagon out of the way to get eggs to Germantown before the train to Lincoln pulled away on the one-track line. Leave straight roads straight.

Washington Irving, in his book *Salmagundi*, emphasizes the good effect of having roads laid out on a grid, and road builders in my part of the world have followed his advice:

> I am clearly of the opinion that this humdrum regularity has a vast effect on the character of its inhabitants, and even on their looks, "for you will observe," writes Likcum, "that they are an honest, worthy, square, good-looking, well-meaning, regular, uniform, straight-forward, clockwork, clear-headed, one-like-another, salubrious, upright kind of people, who always go to work methodically, never put the cart before the horse, talk like a book, walk mathematically, never turn but at right angles, think syllogistically . . . whereas the people of New York – God help them – tossed about over hills and dales, through lanes and alleys, and crooked streets, – continually mounting and descending, turning and twisting – whisking off at tangents, and left-angle triangles, just like their own queer, odd, topsy-turvy, rantipole city, are the most irregular, crazy-headed, quicksilver, eccentric, whim-whamsical set of mortals that ever were jumbled together in this uneven, villainous, revolving globe."

God knows we wouldn't want to be thought eccentric or whimwhamsical in the Bohemian Alps, but the world needs to understand that once we bend a road around a quarry, it's going to stay bent. Forever.

On the high ground of the eastern rim, a young couple has moved into a hundred-year-old frame house. You can see it for miles. The older half of the quarry is within their property line. They have a couple of boys, maybe seven and nine years old. I was there the other day to drop off an antique bed their mother had bought from me, and I told the boys about the sharks' teeth and drew a picture of one so they'd know what to look for. Their mother cheerfully said to me before I drove away, "You know, they told us they're going to straighten this road again."

A handful of people in Garland have formed a committee to restore the little Germantown Bank. It closed nearly seventy years ago and from time to time was used for storage, but until now nobody's thought to bring it back to something like it was when new. It would make a handsome community center, a place for seniors to have coffee and tell stories and play cards. Maybe we'll have a lending library and a display of historical photographs and documents.

Though it's a fine little building, built of gray limestone with four fluted columns out front, and though it's enough of a treasure to be listed on the National Register of Historic Places, the idea of restoring it has been a hard sell in a community where the notion of change sets off the fire whistle. For each one of us shoveling debris out of the cellar, there is somebody else, with his elbows holding down a table, who'd just as soon see the bank torn down. As the Bohemians say, "Wisdom is easy to carry but difficult to load."

The bank needs plenty of work, and it's hot, dirty work in midsummer. The tarred roof leaked for years, and the fancy plaster details – egg-and-dart moldings and elaborate friezes with curly acanthus vines that every few feet turn into leaping fish – almost melted away. The windows are loose in their frames, and the panes are loose in the windows. The interior marble was stripped from the lobby walls and sold long ago. The stairs to the small second floor office have collapsed like a tower of cards, and the cellar is full of old washing machines, implement parts, and rotting boards. The wiring is shot, the plumbing is clogged, and a Virginia creeper, like something out of "Jack and the Beanstalk," has grown up from the cellar and blocked the chimney. A fountain of leaves comes out where the smoke of a furnace should.

47

We've been raising money for labor and materials, and we've received some generous cash donations from local families who appreciate history. A couple who admire what we're trying to do brought their equipment out from Lincoln, soda-blasted the outside clean, and didn't charge us a cent. It would have cost ten thousand dollars if we'd had to pay.

We've raffled off a couple of handsome patchwork quilts made by friends of our project, and we sold tickets on a 1949 Chevrolet pickup I donated. Just recently, we held a fundraising ice cream social with rows of homemade pies displayed on folding tables set up on the sidewalk in front of the bank. Close to a hundred people showed up. While the women who served the pie and ice cream discussed the fortunes of their distant sons and daughters, men in their seventies and eighties, wearing Sunday neckties, sat at tables inside, among the dusty ladders and scaffolding, and told one another what they remembered about the Germantown Bank, or at least what they thought they remembered. As Mark Twain once said, "I have arrived at an age at which the things I remember most clearly never happened at all."

There's an empty house in a field near where I live. Five generations have plowed and planted as close to this flower of somebody's dream as their horses and tractors would go without hooking a corner and pulling it down, and now the declaration of its emptiness, delivered with no more emotion than a man on the early morning radio reading the market news, broadcasts a flat two hundred yards to the county road without touching a single contradiction – no clothesline post or pump or lilac bush – except for the trees that grew up like weeds beside its foundation and that, pressing against it, hold it as hands might hold a peony on Memorial Day, at graveside, in stiff wind, to keep its loose petals from falling away.

You can't dig up wild roses and take them away from their work. They sag in gardens, starved for a gravel road, the hot summer wind, and cracked clay of a ditch. They don't want to be pretty or fragrant or to get too close to one another. Wearing their stained white aprons and moth-eaten pink dresses, each has a few red rose hips to bake and get frosted by state fair time. That's all they care about. If it was good enough for their mothers, it's plenty good enough for them.

Spring
Summer
Autumn
Winter

The Grim Cemetery – yes, that's its name – sits on a low hill a few miles west of the Bohemian Alps. It's surrounded by cornfields and beanfields and fronted by a thick row of shaggy evergreens that toss in the wind. You can see the elevator at Garrison to the northeast.

There's an opening in the evergreens for a gate, and from a chain between tall gateposts hangs a piece of quarter-inch sheet iron about three feet long and two feet high, into which someone with an acetylene torch has cut the letters GRIM CEMETERY, the GRIM large in an arc and the CEMETERY in smaller letters below. The centers of the RS are gone, having fallen out as soon as the torch made its circuit. I'd guess they're lying on the dirt floor of a shed on one of the farms you can see in the distance. The morning sun pours through these two substantial holes in the RS and squeezes through the thin strokes of the rest of the letters.

A couple of Grims are buried here, Emma and Charles. They have a big granite monument and perhaps were the wealthiest people in this area. Near their stone is a small plywood sign that says: POISON IVY AREA. Leaves of Three, Let them Be.

There are about a hundred other graves, covered with prairie sod dense as a rattan doormat. Here lie some of the pioneer Woolseys, Darnells, Hallenbergers, Wyngars, Thurmans, Zimmermans, Pillars, and Whetsels. The most recent burial, one of the Dallegges, is dated in the 1950s, but most of the graves are much older, dating back into the late nineteenth century. Quaint old given names: Zerelda, Sumner, Lottie.

Some of the headstones, cut from soft white marble, are no longer readable. Others have toppled off their bases and have been picked up and lugged over and leaned with a light knock against one of three ancient red-barked pines spaced from north to south. Trees like these are always full of wind. There is never a still day, even in still midsummer, for a tree in a cemetery. They just have to keep talking.

I've driven here today to have another look at the graves of the Weber family, which to me have so much to say about the hardships of life in the last years of the nineteenth century. There are four stones in one row and one in another.

49

I'll let you read them for yourself:

Spring

Summer

Autumn

Winter

EDDIE WEBER

Born Oct. 28, 1892

Died May 20, 1897

Gone but not forgotten

Next, side by side on one stone:

FREDDIE WEBER   FRANKIE WEBER

Born Feb. 11, 1884   Born Mar. 20, 1888

Died May 17, 1897   Died May 17, 1897

Gone but not forgotten

HERMAN WEBER

Born Jan. 30, 1895

Died July 23, 1899

Gone but not forgotten

MINNIE WEBER

Wife of John Weber

Born Oct. 26, 1848

Died Feb. 8, 1895

Gone but not forgotten

And ten feet away, in another row:

JOHN WEBER

Born Feb. 6, 1841

Died Oct. 5, 1913

Gone but not forgotten

First came Freddie, in 1884, when his mother was thirty-five. Then Frankie, when she was thirty-nine; then Eddie, two days after her forty-fourth birthday, then Herman, when she was forty-six. Herman was just nine days old when his mother died, and John was left with Freddie, Frankie, Eddie, and the baby. As the Bohemians would say, "A house without a woman is a meadow without dew."

Then, two years after his wife died, John lost Freddie and Frankie on the same day and Eddie three days later, in May, when the lilacs would have been just beginning to bloom. It was time to get the corn in, but the boys were gone. Lilacs on their coffins, you can bet on it. Then, two years later, little Herman was gone. "When Death goes to the market, he buys up everything he sees."

Their father lived another sixteen years.

Freddie, Frankie, and Eddie probably died of one of the epidemics of the 1890s, diphtheria or whooping cough or even influenza. Minnie probably died from complications of childbirth, but we can't know that. We don't know what happened to little Herman. We'd have to knock at a lot of old screen doors to find out what went wrong.

A woodpecker taps her automatic pencil on the roof of the house, trying to get the lead to drop down through the tube. She is a certified public accountant, dressed appropriately in black and white, and her task is to keep track of a franchise of ants. The roof is her desk, and the shingles her worksheets. So delicious are the tiny, neat entries, and there is never an end to her work.

The sky is like old blue denim just before dawn, with one round hole worn through, exposing the cold bony knee of the moon. I have been hearing the trilling of tree frogs. That a frog – even one with the chirp of a bird – would live in a tree (not even in but on), clinging with little suction cups to keep from falling, is the height of craziness, but forty feet in the air, light as leaves, their tiny hearts are slow and steady under kite paper skin, and their black eyes shine with moonlight. Let us praise all who ascend to such high places on the sheer face of the world.

Today I put on a cowboy shirt my mother made for me when I was fourteen. It still fits, though the style is quaint. It's red with a white yoke and white cuffs, and the yoke and cuffs are embroidered with plump green cacti. It's the kind of shirt Roy Rogers wore for the Saturday matinees when I was a boy. Long ago I lost my long-barreled pearl-handled cap pistols and wore out the boots with the stars.

Mother made most of our clothes when my sister and I were small, and nearly all of her own. One of the most difficult moments we faced after she died was carrying armloads of her handmade suits and jackets and skirts into a charity thrift shop. And then turning our backs on them. I kept her black Singer with its strap of green felt around the neck, with pins and needles waiting and ready. And the sewing basket my Grandfather Kooser bought for her at an auction when I was a baby.

Spring
Summer
Autumn
Winter

Mother was working as a salesgirl when she met my father, but when they were married, she became a full-time homemaker and never went back to salaried work. My father was never a highly paid man, and in dime store spiral notebooks, she kept track of every cent they spent from 1936 till the day she died. The hospital bill, ten days for Mother and me when I was born, was $47.38.

For almost twenty years after my father was gone, she lived alone in their house. With the taste for frugality she'd learned in the Great Depression, she saved what she could from Dad's modest pension and her own small social security checks. She invested in CDs, watching the newspaper to catch the best rates, and slowly amassed nearly a half million dollars, far more than the sum of my father's income for all the years he'd worked.

I asked her one day if she ever went out to eat, and she said, "Yes, when Colonel Sanders has that two-piece chicken special, I'll pick one up. Then I eat one piece that day and the other piece the next." Even with all that money in the bank, she liked to see if she could talk her doctors out of free samples of prescription drugs.

Perhaps fifteen years ago I was visiting with her long distance, and she told me she'd just finished another crazy quilt. She made about ten of these, handsome, featherstitched along the patches but not quilted, tied instead, like comforters. She made them from garage sale fabric scraps. She told me that because she'd already given a quilt to each member of our family, she didn't know what to do with this one. I asked her how much she had in it, and without a pause she said, "Twelve dollars and forty-three cents."

I said, "Why don't you figure out how much you'd like to have for it, maybe seventy-five or a hundred dollars, and I'll buy it from you."

"Why would you do that?" she asked.

I told her I had an old girlfriend who had recently been married and I

52

hadn't yet given her a wedding gift. Mother paused for no more than a breath and then said, "Ted, that's too much to give to an old girlfriend." And she wouldn't let me buy the quilt. I didn't argue. The Bohemians say, "Never blow in a bear's ear."

Spring
Summer
Autumn
Winter

She sold her house a few months before she died and moved into an apartment. On swollen feet neatly tucked in businesslike shoes, with bad lungs wheezing her up and down care center steps, she shopped for her last best deal. Once she found the place she liked, she was happy there, in part because she had enough CD earnings to pay her rent without touching the capital. That had been set aside for my sister and me and our sons.

It was like her to die the day before the rent was due. Just a week before, she'd said to my sister, "The minute I'm gone, you and Ted get my things out of here. We don't want to pay them any extra." You can't discount her choice of that "we." She knew she'd be guiding us even in death. She walks beside me through every store I enter, saying, "Do you really *need* that?"

Her apartment was in an assisted living complex, with three levels of care. The tenants on the lower floor, where Mother lived, had the least expensive quarters and services. The second floor was for more attentive care, equivalent to that of a nursing home. The third floor was for Alzheimer's patients, some of whom stood at the windows looking down into the parking lot.

Despite the fact that Mother was eighty-nine and unable to walk from her chair to the bathroom without sitting down to rest, she persuaded the management to admit her at the least expensive level. It was an example of her extraordinary bargaining skills that they bought into this when they knew from her papers that her heart was enlarged and failing, her lungs were down to 10 percent capacity, and she was tethered full time to an oxygen machine.

At the minimum level of care, renters were encouraged to get engaged in social activities – card games, crafts, and group entertainments – but Mother let them know she had no interest in that. You were also to take your meals in a common dining room, but within a few hours she'd convinced them to bring her a tray. From her first day there, the only times

53

she stepped into the hall were the three or four times she had to be taken to doctors' offices.

Spring
Summer
Autumn
Winter

I'd seen her drive hard bargains all my life, but try as I might, I never got the hang of it. When she was younger and still able to drive, I'd walked beside her as she entered a Ford dealership, wearing her powder blue Mamie Eisenhower pillbox hat and holding her matching purse in both hands. Without ever raising her voice, she talked the dealer into selling her a new Ford for about three-fourths of the sticker price. And she paid for it out of her purse. Several years after that, in the wood-paneled office of a funeral director, with my father's body under a sheet in an adjacent room, she cut a good deal on the price of his cremation. To every amenity the man proposed, she said, "We won't be needing that." When she signed the paper, her lips trembled a little, but she took a deep breath, set her jaw, and got ready for the rest of her life.

A shirt she made has lasted forty-five years.

I have been sitting outside tonight getting the very old news from the stars: what happened to them a hundred million years ago. I followed their lesson, of course, and now I ache all over from being reminded of how small and insignificant I am, that life is as brief as a spark, etc. The universe is always so patronizing, like a high school guidance counselor, like Woodrow Wilson looking down on the world through twinkling glasses, pursing his lips, knowing his history.

Compared to the dreary life of any star, flaring up to collapse into nothing, my life is rich with happenings. For example, a bat like a small black rag has been fluttering back and forth through the yard light all evening, harvesting the stars of tiny moths, catching one tiny star in its teeth with each pass. They jerkily fly this way and that, but they can't escape this hungry little piece of darkness. Local wonders.

On summer mornings during the war years, my father walked from home to Tilden's Store, where he was an assistant manager. His name was Theodore Briggs Kooser, christened for Theodore Roosevelt, who came through Ames on the Chicago Northwestern when Grandmother Kooser was pregnant. My father was a handsome, gregarious man who was perfectly suited for a lifetime of cheerfully helping customers pick

54

out neckties and dresses and hats. He was happiest bustling about the store, straightening displays, directing customers to this or that. As a boy, he had started his own millinery shop in his grandmother's barn. That had been the day of the wide-brimmed picture hat, loaded with flowers, and he would ask the neighbor women for hats they no longer wanted, refit them with ribbons and feathers and artificial flowers, and then sell them. He would have been about twelve years old.

I adored my father and in the afternoon would wait for him at the living room window, watching for him to turn the corner onto our street. He used to hold me in his arms and dance me around, singing a baby talk song that went "Kootie-woot, kootie," over and over. After more than fifty years, I am sometimes overcome by the sudden memory of the damp heat of his chest and the smell of the starch in his dress shirt.

Once when I was four or five, I stole away from my mother and set out to visit my father at the store. Those four blocks were a very long way for a little boy to travel, and I underwent many fearful trials before I got there – strange, frowning houses to tiptoe past, the deep shadows of trees. I remember especially my fear at finding, beside the fish pool at the Adams Funeral Home (where, with irony, the big electric clock was always a few minutes fast), a sinister stone elf, pitted and lichen-covered, staring blankly into the water. A woman found me crying as I stumbled along Main Street, not knowing quite where Tilden's was, and I tearfully blurted out my name and was taken to my father, who was happy to see me.

On hot June days like this, in the days before air conditioning, it must have felt good to sit in a cellar. A while back, I was down in one on an abandoned farm near here and found the parts of a kitchen chair that over the years had come unglued and fallen apart. In the half-light it looked like a pile of animal bones. Somebody had taken it down there to sit on maybe fifty years ago.

I was down in my own cellar just now and noticed our stack of cookie tins is getting rusty. They circulated in our family for years but are temporarily at rest. It's damp down there, too damp to keep potatoes and onions from sprouting, and the rust is coming on around the edges.

55

Somewhere in every house there's a cookie tin, maybe one with green holly stamped in the tin all around the outside, or one with Santa and his sleigh and reindeer whisking along over the snow, or one with a picture of a quaint little village with candles flickering in the windows of the houses. Inside, they're all the same. You can see your face in the bottom, and there may be a few tiny candy balls and old crumbs you can pick up with the tip of your finger.

You find them on a shelf under the basement stairs, or up in a kitchen cupboard, or stuffed in under the sink. One's sitting in the darkness at the back of a closet with somebody's empty galoshes standing on it, or out in the garage, full of rusty nails or oily sparkplugs. Sometimes they're full of spools of thread or buttons and parked under a sewing machine. They spend their entire careers moving from house to house, from town to town. Yours may be ten years old, or twenty, or even thirty.

Let us praise the good ghosts of cookies! Sugar cookies, of course, cut in the shapes of camels and stars and Santas with packs on their backs, some with colored frosting sprinkled with sweet little balls. Molasses cookies too, big and soft or baked hard and thin and burnt around the edges. Kringla like sweet white pretzels, Rice Krispies bars that gum up your teeth, date pinwheels, pfeffernuesse like tiny sofa pillows. Some not so good, but some perfection.

Of all the things left waiting around the house, cookie tins will wait the hardest. Their purpose is freight and travel, and their next stop is never their last. Even mine, with their rust, will move on someday. An old chair in a cellar can collapse from a lack of expectation, but a cookie tin – even embarrassed, covered with mouse turds – is ready to cheerfully pack up and go.

Theirs is no life for a fretter like me. Sitting on a shelf, empty, next to a roasting pan, a man could get too metaphysical: What if this waiting here is all there is? But a cookie tin doesn't have a care in the world. You have to give them plenty of credit.

❧

This prairie is polished by clouds, damp wads of fabric torn from the hem of the mountains, but every scratch shows, from the ruts the wagons made in the 1850s, to the line on an auctioneer's forehead when he takes off his hat. No grass, not even six-foot bluestem, can cover the weather's hard wear on these stretches of light or these people. But though this is a country shaped by storms – a cedar board planed smooth with the red shavings curled in the west when the sun sets – everywhere you see the work of hands, that patina which comes from having been weighed in the fingers and smoothed with a thumb – houses, sheds, machinery, fences – then left behind, pushed off a wagon to lighten the load, a landscape of litter: the boarded-up grocery store with leaves blown in behind the door screen, its blue tin handle reading RAINBO BREAD; the sidewalk heaved and broken; the horseshoe pits like graves grown over with crabgrass and marked by lengths of rusty pipe; the square brick BANK with its windows gone, even the frames of the windows, its back wall broken down and the rubble shoveled out of the way to make room for a pickup with no engine.

You read how the upright piano was left upright by the trail, the soundboard ticking in the heat, how the young mother was buried and left in a grave marked only by the seat of a broken chair, with her name, Sophora, and the date scratched into the varnish, and only a lock of her hair to go west. There are hundreds of graves like that left in the deep grass, on low rises overlooking the ruts that lead on. I tell you that everything here – the auto lot spread in the sun, the twelve-story bank with its pigeons, the new elementary school, flat as a box lid blown off the back of something going farther on, the insurance agent with his briefcase, the beautiful Pakistani surgeon, all these and more, for some reason, have been too burdensome, too big or too small or too awkward, to make it the rest of the way.

✥

I was in the post office the other morning buying a few stamps, and Bob, our mail carrier, came up from the back room to talk to me. "You know that poem you mailed the other day? The one you pasted on that big flat? Well, it came loose, so I taped it back on for you."

Bob is a good-sized, pleasant man who drives a red Jeep Cherokee fitted out with the steering wheel and foot pedals on the right side where the mailboxes are. He carries mail on a route out of Seward, the county seat, as well as on one that comes out of our little town, Garland.

He told me that what I'd done hadn't been such a good idea. I'd been writing drafts of poems on letter-sized sheets of watercolor paper, then pasting on a typed version, then addressing the back side and sending them to friends as postcards. "A letter got in behind the poem and popped it loose," he said, "so I taped it back on. And I had to put another one of them in a big envelope a while back because it was coming apart. If you keep doing that, you're bound to get some damage."

I thanked him, and later that morning I signed a copy of one of my books of poems, inscribing it "To Bob, for exceptional service," and left it at the post office.

We do get exceptional postal service. That is, on top of our customary expectations for delivery during rain and sleet and hail. It's not unusual to get a call from Iris, the postmistress, saying she's got a package for us but she doesn't want Bob to leave it out by the road in the rain. Could we come in and pick it up or call and tell her when she could bring it out?

Yesterday morning I was up on the road, checking to see if the mail had come, when Bob came rolling over the hill. "I'm glad I caught you," he said, reaching to shake my hand. "I wanted to thank you for that book. I liked it. My wife and I read it and showed it to a friend of ours who read it and liked it too.

"I'm not much of a one for poetry," he said. "But let me ask you something." He looked off down the road and then turned back to me. "It says on the back that you're a 'metaphorical poet,' and we weren't sure just what that meant. Does it mean that you . . . well, you say something that isn't quite real?"

"Well, yes" I said, "in a sense. You know that poem at the first of the book, the one where I describe the lights of cities as seen from an airplane at night as looking like constellations of stars? That's a metaphor."

"I think I get it," he said. He paused and thought for a minute. "It's like if I said, 'the wind is like . . . the wind is like . . .' well . . ." he shook his head and smiled, "you know what I mean."

I nodded to show that I did know; then I shook his hand again, and he handed me my bundle of mail and drove on.

This morning I went to the Cattle Bank in Seward – that's the family name, Cattle – and when I got home, I couldn't find my checkbook. It's a dozen miles to Seward, so I phoned the bank and talked to a woman who works there. I told her what had happened.

"Do you think you lost it inside or outside?" she asked.

"Outside, I think. I was parked over there on the east side of the drive-in bank."

"Just a minute," she said, and she was gone for three or four minutes.

"Ted? Thanks for waiting," she said, a little breathless. "Well, I went outside and looked around in the parking lot, but I couldn't find it. I kicked around in some dead leaves blown up against the curb there. I'm just real sorry. If it doesn't show up pretty soon, be sure to call us."

Now that's what I call personal banking.

Alice is crazy about sticks. She can't run through the yard without snatching up a twig or reaching up to nip at a bush. We had a thunderstorm several nights ago – a manna of fallen branches – and she's been trying to drag as many as she can through the dog door onto the glassed-in porch where she sleeps.

This morning I spent an hour raking up twigs and picking up limbs and piling them into the pickup to be driven over the hill to the brush pile. The springy whiplike boughs from our ancient weeping willow were especially enticing, and while I was trying to pitch them onto the load, Alice would bite down on a trailing end, dig her feet in, and not let go until I tugged it free, leaving her with a mouth full of leaves. Whenever my back was turned, she was busy unloading the truck, standing with her paws on the lowered tailgate and dragging the branches back onto the driveway. Given time, she would have unloaded them all.

So I offer this snapshot of life in the alps north of Garland, Nebraska, on the hot first day of June: a sixty-one-year-old man in bib overalls and a black and white puppy bargaining over a pickup full of sticks and branches, the old guy laughing at the dog and the dog laughing back.

People who depend on good weather for a good life – farmers, their families, and field hands – in country where the sky has pressed the dirt flat and pushed the great forests back under the grass, show us how much the weather weighs. Bent-backed under the leaden skies of winter,

59

round-shouldered under the steel blue skies of summer, in their old age shrunken in height and walking with canes, they show us. And their buildings, put up like props to hold up their part of the sky, show it as well. The barns lean to one side and collapse, the porch roofs hang from the eaves and fall, the outbuildings crumple and drop out of sight in the brush at the edge of the ironed-out fields.

Spring
Summer
Autumn
Winter

So, in little towns all over Nebraska, merchants put up marquees, strong steel marquees to shoulder the weight of the weather, to help people unbend and relax. As we browse through the aisles of those stores, we're supposed to feel lighter, ready to open our wallets and release the swift flight of our dollars. And now they're putting lids on all the shopping malls.

We had five inches of hard rain, a real downpour, and our pond ran over the spillway, spilled a lot of bluegills over the hill, thrilled the bullfrogs, who have been booming ever since, and washed out the pit of the outdoor toilet. Some of what was down there is on its way to Branched Oak Lake.

When my son and I moved the toilet there, we put it too close to the path of the overflow.

After the ground dried out, I talked my friend John into bringing his Bobcat over, and he augered me out a nice big hole about ten feet north of the old one. The water can't reach it in this new location.

Then it was a matter of moving the outhouse.

I was raised by clenched-jawed German-Americans who wouldn't have called for help if a tree had fallen on them. When my mother was in her eighties, she fell in her house and twisted her ankle so badly she said she thought she might faint. Rather than use her cordless phone to call my sister or an ambulance, she crawled across the living room floor, turned the floor fan on, and let it blow in her face so she wouldn't pass out.

I went out one morning and looked the situation over and decided that this was the day to move the building over to the new hole. I'd already asked John to auger the hole, and I didn't want to bother him for help in moving the building. My wife would have helped, of course, but she was at work.

60

The outhouse weighs seven or eight hundred pounds, I'd guess, and I knew I'd have to dig around in my brain for what was left of high school physics.

I climbed to the loft of the barn where I keep my inventory of things to hang onto just in case, and I found a ten-foot length of two-inch plumbing pipe and a couple of long two-by-tens. Using the pipe and a concrete block, I levered up first one side of the building and then the other and set the two-by-tens under the edges to serve as tracks for rollers.

Then I went back up to the loft and found two other pipes, four inches in diameter and long enough to reach from track to track. Using my concrete block and lever, and a few pieces of two-by-four to block it up, I was able to get these pipes positioned under the outhouse. I planned to roll the outhouse along the tracks till I got it over the hole.

With my lever, I began to nudge the building along the two-by-ten tracks. As the rollers worked back toward the trailing end, I had to stop and lever up the building, pull the back roller out, and move it forward.

I eventually got the outhouse rolled over the hole, where I'd built a foundation of railroad ties I'd had lying around. To set the building down on these, I had to figure how to get the rollers out.

So I looked around for another plank and found a two-by-twelve about ten feet long. I placed it over a concrete block and under the leading edge, so that with weight on the far end of the plank, I could lift the edge, rock the building back on the trailing side, and work the rollers out. But there was no way I could be out on the far end of the plank and close enough in to pull the rollers out. I might be good enough at high school physics, but I could only reach so far.

So here's how I did it: I found another concrete block and slid it out along the plank till the leverage tilted the building back. Then, leaving the block where it sat, I was able to pull out my pipes. Then it was just a matter of sliding the block back toward the building till the plank let it settle into place.

That's how I spent the afternoon, entertaining myself. As the Bohemians say, "One does not need to show the way to an old hare."

61

Now over fifteen years old, my old pointer, Buddy, has decided it's too much of an effort to step into the grass to empty his bowels, so he's begun to use the brick sidewalk designed for the entrances and exits of human visitors.

His piles of poop attract a variety of butterflies, and I decided this offered an opportunity to learn something about them. After a futile try at identifying several from a window on the porch, using my guidebook, I decided I needed to get the specimens right under my nose. That is, the butterflies. I needed a net.

So I went to my shop in the barn, bent a hoop of heavy fence wire, duct taped it to a broom handle, and hastily sewed a castoff pair of my wife's pantyhose to the loop. With this contraption held high, I approached the butterflies on what I thought were little cat feet, only to discover that they fluttered away as soon as they saw me. I'd disregarded the obvious fact that to a butterfly, a five-foot-seven-inch man is as big as a tree. "As I did stand my watch upon the hill / I look'd toward Byrnane, and anon me thought / The Wood began to move," said somebody in Macbeth. It was probably just as well that I failed at butterfly catching, because had I succeeded in slapping the pantyhose over one of them, I would have been forced to separate the butterfly from the dog poop into which I would surely have mashed the specimen. I did get close enough to match one butterfly to a picture in the book. It was a red admiral. To successfully identify, from ten feet away, a high-ranking naval officer like that should be considered enough for one summer day. We senior citizens are easily entertained.

Our county seat has a population of about six thousand. It has a fine nineteenth-century courthouse on a green, tree-shaded square surrounded by businesses, the location of Seward's traditional Fourth of July celebration, which thousands attend.

But for some of us, an important part of the twenty-first century will take place not on the public square but at the municipal swimming pool, one of America's few round pools.

After hours, it's the mirror of the world's biggest reflector telescope, collecting the feeble light of distant galaxies and the cold contrails of transcontinental jets, but on this afternoon, at the end of the first week of July 2000, it's a shatter of broken light.

About three hundred people are here, beginning to assemble the *Spring* twenty-first century's memories out of the elemental materials of light *Summer* and skin and water. Each of their recollections of this day will be differ- *Autumn* ent, and some will endure. *Winter*

It's ninety-four degrees, light shining like sun block on the leaves of the maples outside the chain link fence. Shade splashes out over the hoods of the cars at the edge of the parking lot. Beyond them, the pavement is hot and as white as spilled popcorn.

The grass in the park is cut; yellow jackets buzz in paper cups in the trash barrels. A few days ago, the town's Fourth of July fireworks rocketed into heads of red and green punk rock hair, dripping glittering earrings of flame, and now, here and there in the dusty grass, you can see scraps of gray paper that held those wild curls in place all the way from Taiwan.

The round pool is, to those here, the center of the world. A circle is the ultimate in order, and despite the chaos of splashing and squeals, the loud country music protesting the world's unfairness, despite the lifeguards' heys! and whirring whistles, the PA system honking like a goose call, this dancing, laughing crystal illustrates a pure and godly order.

At its center is the largest group, the youngest among us, all elbows, runny noses, and mischief. A little farther from the center is a slightly smaller group, quieter children at the edge of puberty, skinny, trying out poses, watching one another without pretending not to.

On the edge of the pool are the teens, a still smaller group, the girls in tanned and glistening clutches, all gold and bronze, all legs and hair, wearing their towels like skirts. The boys are thin and white and wet, and as they walk the pool's hard edge, they keep their shoulders back and their eyes averted.

¯ Still inside the fence are a few young mothers with unhappy toddlers, the women struggling with the blue nylon and colored plastic baggage of motherhood, the toddlers struggling with their awkwardness. Then there are a few older people who sit apart, their hands and bottoms spread flat on their towels.

Beyond the fence, on benches under the trees, is the smallest group, my group, consisting of me, with my notebook, and three white-haired women, two of whom are interested in what is going on in the pool and the other who is buried cross-legged in a novel with one foot bobbing to some beat she feels or hears.

And such is the order of this place, this center of a galaxy spreading us out in a spiral: The most and the youngest crowded into the hot bright middle, dense with fevers, the fewest and the oldest of us waiting in the thinning oxygen of the outer circle. In the unknown beyond us, the sound of Country Froggy 98 fades, the phone call for Ted Hotovy goes unanswered, and everybody's sunny afternoon in Seward spins happily into the realm of memory.

Today, at a garage sale, I found a cigar box of miniature glass animals: a couple of horses with broken legs, a penguin with a missing wing, an elephant without a trunk. They took me home to Iowa.

Several years ago, I got up the courage to knock at the door of 109 West Ninth Street, Ames, Iowa, where we lived when I was a child. I hadn't been in the house for nearly forty years. I told the owner, a young man who taught film studies at Iowa State University, who I was, and he invited me in. He had heard of my uncle Tubby, who in his position at the university had collected a vast library of unique industrial films. I met the man's wife and two young redheaded daughters. He took me through the house. At the entrance to each room, a brass doorknob shone as if still waiting for my father's hand to come and turn it, and for his voice to call into the darkness to wake me up for breakfast.

When I was living in that little house, my friends and I invented a game called Miniature Animals. We'd buy tiny glass creatures at the five-and-dime and then dream up fantastic adventures for them. My friend Billy had a set of wooden blocks his father had made, and we constructed elaborate castles where these adventures were staged. We played for hours. From Uncle Tubby's elephant collection, he gave me a small china elephant that I named Pinky. Pinky had especially spectacular adventures because I was the kind of child to make up things. My friends were envious.

Pinky disappeared one day, and I was never able to find him. Several years ago, one of my playmates, Larry, now a middle-aged man, confessed that he'd stolen Pinky and buried him under his front porch. He hadn't been able to stand it that Pinky had such an exciting life. Of course, my next animal, Tux the Penguin, took right up where Pinky had left off, sallying forth on unsurpassed adventures. It hadn't helped to bury Pinky.

The man who now owns my house told me that when he'd replaced the back stoop, his daughters had found "a lot of tiny glass animals" in the dust beneath it.

The years have been kind to another white bungalow at the back of my mind, with its bay window like a mirror in the morning sun and its green wooden plant box crowded like Noah's ark with the anxious faces of pansies. No wear or tear has taken that house from me, though it has been years since I last saw it and even more years since my father pointed it out to me, saying "That's where the artist Velma Rayness lives. She paints her pictures there, behind that window."

I never met her, never saw her, never saw a picture she painted, as far as I can remember. She was out and among us, of course, buying her groceries, living a life, but no one ever told me which of the many middle-aged women in our town she was. She taught art lessons, and though I was interested in painting and drawing, I never thought to ask my parents for a lesson. No different from most children, I didn't like lessons of any kind. I didn't like old people with cold hands and sour breath telling me what to do. Not even the elusive Miss Rayness, as my father described her. But her life, as I imagined it to be, intrigued me always.

In nearly every little town, there is a man or woman who paints pictures of dogs and horses and pots of daisies, and that person is almost always spoken of with pride. A person with any kind of talent is held in high regard in places like Ames, Iowa, or Garland, Nebraska.

It's that same community regard that drives the popular "crafts" industry. Villages all over the country are full of people busily jigsawing out wooden geese with sunbonnets or painting heart-shaped knick-knack shelves. Pale blue. There's nothing wrong with that. We want to earn the affection of our neighbors. I too have always wanted to make something special, to have the admiration of my community. I've spent my life trying to move myself into a house just like the one where Velma Rayness lived.

Spring
Summer
Autumn
Winter

We have a way of getting by in Nebraska, a way of making do. My good friend Bob Hanna, an artist who lives in Lincoln, had an ancient bachelor uncle, Louie, for whom he had been appointed guardian. Uncle Louie lived in the veteran's home in Grand Island, about two hours west, and when he died in his nineties, his body was taken to Gibbon, Nebraska, about an hour still farther west, for cremation, because Gibbon has the nearest crematorium. On the morning of the funeral, I saw Bob on the street. He looked hurried. He said he and his wife had to leave in a few minutes for Gibbon, where they were to pick up Uncle Louie's ashes and return them to Grand Island in time for the funeral.

An hour later I saw Bob again and asked why he hadn't left yet. He said: "When I got back to my office, I had a phone call from the crematorium at Gibbon. The man there said, 'Bob, there's no sense in you having to drive all the way out here to pick up your uncle's ashes. There's an auto parts truck coming through this morning, and we'll just put the ashes on that. They can drop them off in Grand Island.'"

Uncle Louie would have thought that was fine.

The Bohemians say, "A loan often comes home crying." That's why it's so hard to borrow a tool in these hills. One of the worst offenses imaginable is to borrow a tool and then return it dull or broken. The next worst offense is to never return it at all. In the latter instance, at least, the owner doesn't have to suffer the insult of the tool's abuse, just its permanent absence.

I got burned early. Shortly after we moved to the alps, a neighbor borrowed one of my extra lawn mowers, a three-horse model with big wheels on the back, good for mowing over bumpy ground. She kept it a while, then loaned it to somebody else a little farther up the road, who said he needed it for just a day.

Weeks went by, and I eventually asked what had happened to it, and the first borrower said that, oh, she'd loaned it to so-and-so, who said he'd bring it back that next day but hadn't. I told her I'd like to have it back. She then approached the second borrower, who said, oh, was that old machine Ted's? Well, it had quit working, so he took it to the land-fill. I spent a few days trying to shake some sense back into my head.

Spring
Summer
Autumn
Winter

My closest neighbor, Lindsay French, has a gas-powered posthole au-ger, and I knew better than to ask to borrow it. Besides, he likes to help. So I asked him if he'd help me drill some postholes for a fence. He said some fellows he knew had borrowed his auger and recently brought it back and that he'd be down after he got off work that afternoon.

He and his son Matt got to our place as scheduled, and he carefully lifted the auger out of his pickup bed and looked it over and checked the choke and started it up. But when he set it on the spot where the first hole was to be dug, the clutch wouldn't grab the auger bit and make it turn. He revved it up, but that didn't help. The men who'd borrowed it had burned out the clutch and returned it without saying a word. On the scale of Bohemian Alps misdemeanors, that's a whole lot worse than breaking a window at the Germantown Bank.

Lindsay is a red-haired, big, hard-working man, with freckled fists. He clenched his flushed jaw, and his sideburns stood out as if they were carrying voltage. He slowly lifted the auger and carried it in both arms over to the pickup and laid it gently in the back, as if it were an injured child. He set it among his chains and ropes and pry bars and his other tools with the same care that he was just then using to choose the few strong words he intended to use when he phoned the borrowers.

I saw Matt a couple days after that and asked him what had happened. He said the new clutch was likely going to cost a couple hundred dollars, and then he grinned and said his dad had phoned the men, and they'd agreed to pay for the repairs.

Most Nebraskans aren't ready talkers. We hold back a lot more stories than we ever let out. As the Czechs say, "A word which flies out of the mouth like a sparrow cannot be drawn back, even by four horses."

One morning I was chatting with an attractive young woman I know, and I asked her what she'd been up to since I'd seen her last. She said she'd just returned from a funeral in Missouri.

"Oh?" I said, "Somebody in the family?"

"Yes," she said, a little sadly, "My great aunt." She reached up and
swept a lock of hair from her brow. Her fingers are long, with perfectly
cared-for nails.

"Had she been ill for a long while?" I asked.

"No. She had a stroke. It went fast. But she was eighty-seven years
old. She was way into her seventies when she got married," she said.
"Her husband died a couple years ago."

There was a moment of silence, and I broke it by remarking that it
was certainly unusual for a woman to have waited so long to marry.
Most girls of that generation were married in their teens.

She looked into my eyes and paused before she answered. Then she
sighed and began. "She'd been afraid to get married until she was old,"
she said. "When she was a girl, just fifteen years old, a sad thing happened, and it kept her from getting married for years and years." She met
my eyes and looked away.

"Her parents had a hired man on their place, about thirty years old at
the time. He fell in love with my aunt and went to her father to ask for
her. Of course, he had never so much as even let on to my aunt how he
felt, so it came as a complete surprise. She'd never thought much about
him, one way or another. And her father was furious that a plain hired
man, an older man with no money and no prospects, would be so forward, and he ran the man off, told him never to show his face around
there again.

"The man had been sleeping in a tack room in the barn, and he went
down there and gathered his things and walked off without a word. Late
that night, he came back with a shotgun. The family was asleep. He
went into the parents' room, which was on the first floor, and shot them
both where they lay in bed. Then he went upstairs, walked right past my
aunt's closed door, went into the next room, and shot her twin brothers,
who were eleven years old and awake and screaming. Then he walked
past her door again, without even trying the knob, went back down the
stairs and outside. He went down by the windmill, stuck the gun in his
mouth, and shot himself. My great aunt was the only one of the family
to survive. When the shots stopped, she waited a long while before leav-

68

ing her room. Then she found the bodies and ran crying to the neighbors, a mile away, to tell them what had happened."

She paused again and then looked up at me. "Because that happened," she said, "my parents say my aunt was afraid to get married. She got the idea that her being attractive to the hired man had caused the murders. So she waited until she was homely and old. I guess by then she thought it would be safe to let somebody love her. Then nobody could ever get hurt because of her looks. It's funny, because I've seen pictures of her as a girl, and she wasn't even that pretty, really . . ." She touched her cheek with her fingertips.

Spring
Summer
Autumn
Winter

"So, that's where I've been the past few days," she said. She took a deep breath and assembled a smile. "That's where I've been, dealing with that."

Early this morning, when I went down to the barn, I surprised a young opossum assembling its nest. It had a big wad of leaves curled up in its tail and was on its way under the floor of the old feed bunkers. I'd turned on the light and stood nearby to watch it, and it went on about its work as if I weren't there.

Opossums look too much like rats for most people, but I think they're quite handsome, the young ones especially, with busy pink hands, pink noses, and shining black eyes. I hope this one can keep out of reach of my dogs. Alice has caught a couple of young ones I had to rescue from her.

An old barn shelters lots of creatures. There are hundreds of spiders, dozens of beetles. A half dozen yellow-shafted flickers have drilled holes in the siding and live in the loft. The dogs killed a lovely white weasel one winter and left it in the straw for me to find.

Ordinary house mice and white-footed field mice live wherever you might be looking, and if you stand still for just five minutes, you'll see one scamper past. There are hundreds of square feet of old boards and straw and miscellaneous junk in our barn, and the mice have left their seedlike droppings on every inch of it. They own it all.

Snakes follow wherever there are mice, and we have bullsnakes, blue racers, and garter snakes. Bullsnakes are marked a lot like rattlers, and when they get cornered, they'll find a nearby leaf and rattle it with their

69

tail. Blue racers were around long before the age of robotics, but they gleam with aluminum and gold as if made for the future. The bullsnakes and blue racers knot up together during the winter, but the garter snakes stick to their species when it comes to hibernation.

When we first moved to the country, I spent a lot of time getting acquainted with what was here. I was outside the barn one day, peering through a crack in the foundation, when I thought I saw a big metal gear slowly revolving on a vertical axis. What kind of a machine is that, I wondered, something to do with the well? As I watched, it became a big bullsnake moving through a shaft of light, bending itself around a big stone, its spots like cogs.

Snakes get in the barn and enter the language. The Bohemians say of their ancient oppressors, the Germans, "When a snake gets warm on ice, then a German will wish well to a Czech."

When we moved to the country, the loft was full of old hay bales, dried out and dusty, dotted with the nests of mud dauber wasps. I wanted the space for storage for our extra belongings, so one afternoon I set about to fork down the hay, a bandanna tied over my nose and mouth. There's a windmill on the west side of the barn, and the sun was behind it. Suddenly, against the dust in the air, an image of the turning windmill appeared, upside down, maybe four feet high, projected through the lens of a small hole in the barn siding. Old barns are big enough to hold a lot of little miracles.

Kathleen and I recently drove to Germanfest, at Fairbury, about forty miles south of the Bohemian Alps.

Between people in a standing, applauding crowd, I got a glimpse of a girls' precision drill team. They were wearing sequined aqua one-piece swimsuits that sparkled in the light, which fell through the grand old trees of the courthouse square. If you sloshed a bucket of swimming pool water till it flew up over the rim of the bucket, they would look like that, moving as one glittering splash, miraculously held in the air, not falling back, their pretty faces bobbing on the surface. Each had her shining baton, which she pumped up and down and swept through the air, keeping the magic working, keeping the bright wave standing.

70

Earlier, a few miles north of Fairbury, Kathleen and I visited the isolated grave of George Winslow. His stone marker, tall as a man, stands in a field of prairie grass near the faded ruts of the Oregon Trail. Winslow died at twenty-five, on a wet spring morning a hundred and fifty years ago, of fever and chills. The members of his party, who were on their way to find gold, hastily buried him, scratched his name into a red stone from a nearby creek, and left it over his grave. Sixty years later, one of his sons came out from Massachusetts to look for the grave and by luck walked right to the spot, dug down, and found the stone under a foot of sod.

Spring

Summer

Autumn

Winter

The sequined girls of the drill team turned and stomped their feet, then turned in the other direction and stomped again, as if insisting on marking this spot where they marched in the glory of their youth, on their way to somewhere.

A little bit of good comes out of just about everything. The day before yesterday, I dropped a heavy wooden garage door on my head while I was pounding on a stuck roller, and it knocked me flat when the pin in the roller sheared off. It cut up my head a little but would have really done some serious damage if it hadn't been for an old high-backed lawyer's desk that was sitting beneath it and that took most of the weight (a desk I've been wanting to get out of the garage but hadn't yet gotten around to finding another place for).

I wanted to fix the door right away, though we seldom use it. "He who postpones is worse than the lazy." So yesterday I went to Earl Carter Lumber in Lincoln, having been told that they stocked rollers for doors like mine. The person who helped me was a big helpful man in his late fifties and, making conversation while he looked for the parts, he mentioned how good our weather has been. "We'll be pitching horseshoes this weekend," he said. "The kids will be bringing the shoes and stakes." I told him that I had had an uncle with cerebral palsy who couldn't talk well or walk well but who could pitch horseshoes with the best. "Isn't that great!" he said. "You know, I had an uncle who was tri-state horseshoe champion three years running. I asked him one time how I could get as good at it as he was, and he said, 'Son, you got to pitch a hundred shoes a day.'"

That's the good that came out of dropping a two-hundred-pound door on my head, that one line. Anybody who wants to be a writer, or to get good at anything at all, ought to be ready to pitch a hundred shoes a day.

❧

Our friend John is a country entrepreneur. He doesn't make the kind of money that will ever get him profiled in Forbes or Fortune, or even in the Seward County Independent, our weekly paper, but he's every bit as creative in putting together a deal as is Donald Trump, and he doesn't have Trump's insufferable ego. Nor does he have supermodels following him about, of course, but he does have a good-looking black sheepdog named Dude, a handsome son, and a tight little farmhouse heated with wood.

Yesterday evening he came rumbling down our lane in an old International four-wheeler, just stopping by for coffee. He had the concentrated, slightly urgent look of a man with a good idea warming his belly. Maybe two good ideas.

He's a small, solidly built man in his forties with a rugged, heavy face and quick eyes. He's on his feet, back and forth, while he talks – over to the coffee maker and back, over to look out the window and back. He has a hay and feed business and is an experienced horse trader and horse trainer. He also has a tree spade on the back of an old truck for moving trees and a Bobcat with a shear on the front for cutting cedars out of people's pastures.

As a young man he rode as a jockey for a short time on the tracks in Montana and was a groom on a Long Island estate where Edward Albee and Andy Warhol sometimes visited, though John didn't know who they were until years later.

During the past few years the racehorse business has fallen on hard times due to the introduction of other kinds of gambling, and John's pretty much dropped out of horse dealing. But he keeps a few around for trading stock. The saying goes, "An old horse must die in somebody's keeping." You can be certain John's not to be the last in line.

Mostly he makes his living buying and selling hay and feed. This takes hours and hours of driving around in the country, burrowing and snuffling like a badger into stacks of bales only to surface with a fistful of mildewed alfalfa to prove that it isn't worth the price the seller wants. And also to warn that if the bales aren't sold at once, at a much lower price, to him, the whole pile will rot where it stands. Will melt down like a nuclear pile. I've seen these sellers standing with their fists hanging like stones at their sides and their eyes on their boots. Growing and mowing and storing hay is work enough without having to bargain with John.

During the past few years he's expanded his hay and feed business into selling and distributing bedding straw at fairs and livestock shows around the Midwest. He sets up camp in a barn at the fairgrounds and delivers clean straw to the animal barns. He also sells custom feeds. If the Budweiser Clydesdale horses are scheduled for an appearance, for example, John is the man who can find, buy, and deliver the baled timothy these coddled giants like to eat, no small matter in a state where very little timothy is grown.

There's always a new deal brewing. Last night we were told about the potential for making good money at a highbrow stock show in Kansas City. It seems that the Kansas City people need bedding material, "mulch," as John calls it, and he's figured out a way of getting it to them and then getting rid of it for them once the animals have gone.

We've learned to let these stories come at us from several different directions, and this time we were first told about giant salvage yards in the city, full of wooden shipping pallets. The people that run these yards are paid to pick up the used pallets from factories, and the pallets then collect in enormous piles in dumps. They can't be burned, due to air pollution laws, and they can't be used as lumber, because the boards are full of staples.

John plans to offer to dispose of the pallets, charging so much for each, thus ridding the pallet dumps of their mounting problem. Then, with a tub grinder, he plans to grind the pallets into chips. He'll fasten magnets on the exhaust chute that will draw off the staples as the chips fly past.

Then he'll deliver the wood chips as bedding for the animals at the stock show, charging so much per animal, enough to pay for the transportation of the pallets, the grinder, and his help, plus, he smiles, a little profit.

When the stock show is over, he'll load up the used wood chips,

73

soaked with horseshit and urine, and sell them to local nurseries as fertilized mulch. That's where the word *mulch* finally gets justified, though he's been using it to describe the chips since long before his narrative got to Kansas City.

And it's good publicity for the stock show people, he remarks, giving them the opportunity to talk up their recycling activity while the animal rights activists look on from a distance.

And as if this weren't enough to follow, over a couple cups of coffee, we were then treated to yet another idea – a business that John and a friend of his in Omaha would start, a dry cleaning service in which they would position lockers in apartment complexes. The people who live there would put their dirty clothes in the lockers with their checks, and John and his partner would pick up the clothes, get them cleaned, and return them to the lockers the next day. It'd take a truck, of course, and maybe four thousand bucks for the lockers . . .

"We'll do for dry cleaning what Godfather's has done for pizza!" he laughed, slapping his sides, completely delighted. Out on the porch, our dogs barked in response, and my wife and I sat back and silently wondered if we would ever get a good idea. It's an inspiration to have John drop by, and as the Czechs say, "Wherever the horse rolls, it leaves some of its hair."

The weekly newspaper published in our county seat arrived by mail today, and I've just read about a woman from a nearby town who recently attended a Women In Agriculture conference in Kearney. The conference provided "farm women with valuable information, while giving them a chance to meet counterparts from across the state." The use of the word *counterparts* suggests that the 452 women who attended, divided into two ranks, were lined up facing one another and then encouraged to share "common experiences." That's something I wish I could have seen.

But I was even more interested in this description of a workshop that was offered: "The class discussed how you can relate to somebody else and verbalize feelings without having them shut down. There is a way to encourage others to remain receptive, even though it may not be what they want to hear." Tonight, in the pale gray light of a late summer dusk, in farmhouse kitchens all over Nebraska, you can hear the slow scraping sound as hundreds of women pull up their chairs and sit down opposite their husbands, those full-time counterparts, and you can see those husbands putting both hands around their coffee cups and squeezing them a little while they listen to some carefully thought out words of sharing, which they may not want to hear.

The gravel road runs west past a grove of dying cottonwoods, leaning, creaking, swinging their armbones and shinbones. Pieces of wrinkled cottonwood skin lie in the grass. The death of a tree comes at the end of a very protracted disease. No sudden ruptures of the heart.

It is late August, the sun bending south and the shadows long and cool and precisely the color of the sky, not the sky above, which is pale and cobwebby with clouds, but the clear blue sky at the horizon. September is out there, thirty miles away, an intense blue ring all around the horizon, circling this last shrinking pool of summer through which I am driving, my elbow out in the breeze, wind in my hair, big summer-green grasshoppers landing baffled on the windshield. My pup, Alice, watches the road with more eagerness than would any man or woman. The windshield and the window on her side of the pickup are dotted with smears from her nose.

At first I thought I was seeing cottonwood leaves caught between layers of the wind, unable to fall to the ground, but they were butterflies, orange-and-black Monarchs beginning to gather for their fall migration, perhaps 150 of them. Surely nobody really believes these frivolous flyers can make it all the way to the south before the first frost. Their migration is altogether casual. Monarchs stroll in the air. It takes them a whole day to cross one forty-acre field of beans because they go forward and back, up and down, side to side, alighting here and there like the hands of shoppers above a table of sale merchandise, not knowing quite what to touch next.

Autumn

Do not choose your wife at a dance,
but on the field amongst the harvesters.

The first official morning of autumn, sunny, cool, and breezy, the leaves just beginning to fall. The cottonwoods that lean above our country road have started to pitch their gold coins into the beds of passing pickups, but the elms and hackberries and oaks stubbornly cling to fistfuls of green.

The last of the barn swallows have finally set out for the south. During the past few weeks I've been keeping an eye on four hatchlings in a nest under the eaves on the west side of the house. We had a half dozen nests on the house and in the barn this summer, and each set of parents raised one hatch of young birds earlier, then a second. These four were the last to be hatched from a second setting and were slow to accept their flight orders. They were well past the stage of keeping their beaks open all day begging for food and had begun to squat with their chins on the mud rim, wearing the self-conscious expressions you see on human infants when they have just filled their diapers. The rest of the swallows, some of which are undoubtedly related to the nestlings – uncles and aunts and cousins born here in seasons past – were impatient to get started on their migration (they are usually on their way south by Labor Day), and the adults and older siblings flew in wild ellipses, cheeping like rubber bathtub toys, trying to encourage the young ones to take just one chance on the air. Then the adults would alight on the power line, waiting to see what would happen. And the young ones would fly, just a little, then quickly flutter back to the solid gray cement of their nest. It's been getting down into the forties during the nights, and I thought they'd better get moving soon, or the rest of the family would brand them as incorrigible and abandon them. I can remember being threatened with that as a small child: "If you don't get dressed right now, Teddy, we'll have to leave you behind!" I must have gotten dressed in time because they never left me. And this morning the little birds and their parents are gone.

Huge flocks of geese were everywhere in old Bohemia.

Our word *gossamer* comes from the Middle English *gossomer*, or "Goose Spring Summer," which is that time of the year when spiders build their nests Summer in the grass and strands of spun silk are plucked up by the wind to sing Autumn in the light like mandolin strings.

Winter Now autumn has come to Seward County, the wild geese are honking overhead, and our apple tree is heavy with fruit. In thirteenth-century Scotland, the botanists could not be swayed from their belief in the elusive goose tree, which could be found at the heart of the forest and which bore geese as its singular (and noisy) fruit.

And, on a cool autumn evening with the dust of the harvest yellowing the full moon, I have been reading in an old book that the shearing of the last portion of grain was called "cutting the gander's neck" and betokened a winter of plenty.

There are a couple of traditional American patchwork designs honoring geese, "Geese in the Pond" and "Goose Tracks," both lucky charms, unlike the malign pattern called "Turkey Foot," which had so bad an influence on behavior that no child was permitted to sleep beneath it for fear he or she would grow up disoriented and unstable.

The in-laws of a friend of mine live in Saline County, the next county south of us and the home of many Czechs. They live in the country and keep geese. One afternoon, an old woman wearing a shawl came to the back door. She was a neighbor, known for her home remedies. She had come, she said, because she was making a special salve, and she needed "the green end of a goose turd."

It was on a Goose Summer day in 1783 when Thomas Bewick observed a drove of nine thousand geese passing through Chelmsford on their way to London:

> To a stranger it is a most curious spectacle to view these hissing, cackling, gabbling, but peaceful armies, with grave deportment, waddling along (like other armies) to certain destruction. The drivers are each provided with a long stick at one end of which a red rag is tied as a lash, and a hook is fixed at the other: with the former, of which the geese seem much afraid, they are excited forward; and with the latter, such as attempt to stray, are caught by the neck and kept in order: or if lame, they are put into a hospital cart, which

usually follows each large drove. In this manner they perform their journeys from distant parts, and are said to get forward at the rate of eight or ten miles a day, from three in the morning till nine at night.

You may recall that in the *Odyssey,* Penelope kept twenty geese for her entertainment while Odysseus was wandering. In a nightmare, she watched as an eagle killed her beloved flock, and she was disconsolate. The dream eagle told her that he was Odysseus come home at last and that the geese were the lovers who had besieged her in his absence. Later, when she related this dream to Odysseus (who was disguised to keep her from recognizing him), he agreed with the eagle's interpretation, to which dear Penelope replied, "Dreams are awkward and confusing things" – why should the geese she loved be the symbols of the lovers she so bitterly despised? Despised? The question as to how deeply Penelope resented those attentive lovers is, after hundreds of years, still a matter of conjecture, but I think that, surely, it is Odysseus who may be the goose in this tale, wearing his Goose Summer Halloween costume and believing his wife doesn't know who she's talking to. Two old proverbs: "A goose is a goose still, dress it as you will." And, "Feather by feather the goose is plucked."

On certain Saturdays in our own Goose Summer, it is possible to see as many as seventy-five thousand people parading toward Memorial Stadium in Lincoln to watch the Nebraska Cornhuskers play football. As on those great goose drives of two hundred years ago, during which red rags were used as goads, each football fan wears something red, the team's official color. Go Big Red! Few of the participants in this noisy gaggle have any idea they are honoring the goose. The dreamy goose girls and the coarse drovers have gone to their graves, and gone is the memory of those long and dusty drives when the loose goose-down floated like milkweed cotton on the autumn breeze. But the hospital carts are still in attendance.

The following is from "Managing the Home Goose Breeder Flock," published by the Cooperative Extension Service, Institute of Agriculture and Natural Resources of the University of Nebraska:

One of the most frequent questions about geese is how can you tell the differ-ence between males and females? This question is difficult to answer. The

81

only sure way, and even this requires some practice, is by examining the re-
productive organs. This process is quite accurate when the necessary skill has
been obtained. Catch and lift the goose by the neck and legs. Lay it on its
back on a table or over your bended knee, with the tail pointed away from
you. Place the tail of the bird far enough over the edge so it can be readily
bent downward. Then insert your index finger into the cloaca about 1/2
inch. Move your finger around in a circular manner several times to relax
the sphincter muscle which encloses the opening. Sometimes a little vaseline
on your finger helps accomplish this job.

Here I interrupt to ask the author, if he thinks this procedure requires some skill, how much skill does it take to explain what you and the goose are doing when your spouse comes into the room?

According to the TV weatherman – all smiles at six this morning – today is to be one of the "top ten days of the year!" He was exclaiming his own prediction of good weather, of course, but most of us among his early morning viewers are hoping that this will be a top ten day of the year in ways other than that. I for one am hoping that it will be among the top ten days for making a few pints of applesauce from our bruised and wormy windfalls and also among the top ten days for gluing together my late mother's cutting board, which during the past week split in half and by so doing opened a crack in my heart, into which a good deal of syrupy sentiment trickled.

Mother would never have paid "good money," as she would have said, for a gourmet cutting board, heavy and thick as a layer cake and cleverly fitted together from finely planed strips of chocolate-dark and sugar-light hardwoods. No, her cutting board was three short pieces of one-by-four pine, glued together into a surface about the size of a piece of typewriter paper. She probably bought it at a yard sale. On this crude tablet, which over the years turned roast beef brown from the oil of store brand cheese and the juice from whatever fruit was on sale, was inscribed her kitchen's history, scored into the surface by a dull paring knife with the rivets gone from one side of the handle. There are chapters on flaky pie dough, thick egg noodles, and round steak hammered to a pulp.

82

When she died and my sister and I were dividing her few belongings, I kept Mother's cutting board. At the time I didn't have a sentimental attachment to it, but I thought my wife and I might be able to make some use of it. I hold on to nearly everything that comes my way.

Spring
Summer
Autumn
Winter

And we have used it, nearly every day. It is my generation's time to slice store brand cheddar on it and dice sale carrots and core whatever poor apples might fall from our trees. And I am going to make applesauce today not so much because I like applesauce but because it would please Mother – and, for that matter, her mother and her mother's mother – to know I don't intend to let those miserable little windfalls go to waste.

So, on this top ten day, the first thing I'm going to do is to carry the halves of my mother's cutting board down to my shop in the barn and glue them together. And then I'm going to clamp them to dry – clamp them with heavy iron pipe clamps, tightly, so tightly my fingers hurt twisting the handles, because there is so much I want to hold together.

Beyond the window, a nearly bare tree branch has pushed its fingers into the light, disturbing the surface. The light ripples over a painted wooden chest on the other side of the room as it would ripple over the bed of a shallow stream, and the flowers and birds and little fish painted on the chest drift downstream over the pine yellow sand, into the broad and shining future, a watery mirror beneath which nothing can be clearly seen.

We are always trying to find footing on the damp edge of the future, but to most of us, the dry sand of the past feels firmer under our sneakers. Now in my sixties, I go back and go back.

Earlier, I was out in the barn making a small worktable that I could use in my corncrib art studio. The smell of the new pine boards choked me with wistfulness.

In September 1961, I undertook a stint of student teaching at the high school in Marshalltown, Iowa. I was engaged to be married, and my fiancée's parents, who lived in Marshalltown, generously let me have her vacant room. She was then in her sophomore year at Iowa State and living in a sorority in Ames, about an hour's drive away. Her mother was a splendid cook, and her father a good storyteller, and we sometimes sat in their living room and drank beer and talked until late in the evening.

By that time – I was twenty-two – I was certain that I wanted to be a writer, but I ached all over with the melancholy prospect of facing countless years of acting like a grown-up. Writing poems and stories was exhilarating, and I could not foresee any such fun under the ghastly burden of steady employment. Teaching English was the only solution that had thus far presented itself, offering as it did the promise of days spent talking about books and writing. But I was painfully shy and dreaded every moment spent in front of groups of people. Most of the time my intestines were tied in such tight knots that my voice trembled and squeaked.

My borrowed room was on the second story, with two windows on the south side looking down across the roof of a one-story addition to the house. I mention this because the odor of sun-warmed asphalt shingles is a strong part of my memory of that room. That, and – most pungent in memory – the sweet fragrance of the unfinished pine bookshelves upon which I had placed my books: my Webster's collegiate dictionary, my Oxford anthology of British and American poets, and my textbooks from the high school. My sanctuary. I often stretched out on the bed when I got home from teaching. I'd close my eyes and listen to the warm late afternoon breezes rustle the leaves in the trees below me.

Start out to make a table, and the smell of a pinch of sawdust sweeps you back forty years.

I took a drive north this morning and passed through tiny Bruno, Nebraska, where there's a building on the main street worth seeing. It's on my tour of the wonders of the Bohemian Alps. The building is of your standard storefront grocery model, with one tall window on either side of a single recessed door. Both windows have been covered with sheets of paneling painted an autumn red. On one side of the door a sign says BEAUTY PARLOR and on the other side is TAXIDERMY STUDIO. Once you were in, you'd have to be careful which way you turned.

This is the season when, after a yearlong absence, the antique grain trucks reappear. All day you can see them crawling along the country

roads toward the local grain scales, weighed down over suffering springs
with heaps of corn or soybeans. These postwar Fords and GMCs and
Internationals, sometimes even Studebakers – some of them mottled
green and yellow like unpicked melons, some dusty blue, some red-go-
ing-to-brown – have long, comical, out-of-place faces from the 1940s,
faces with tiny headlight eyes and the low-slung smiles of chrome
bumpers, looking as if they belong in children's books.

Since last year's harvest, they've been waiting in the deep weeds behind barns and machine sheds, leaking brake fluid, dotted by pigeon
lime, their windshields getting that oily, old glass, rainbow look. Spiders
and moths have foolishly trusted in immobility and silence and have
draped each truck with cobwebs and stuffed convenient cracks with co-
coons, right down to the tread in the tires. But now, with noisy mufflers
and with young mice in their cracked upholstery, each truck has been
gassed up and greased up and laboriously jump-started to be sent wobbling and bellowing into the fields to be filled by enormous new combines that cost as much as a house. When loaded nearly to the point of
collapse, they lurch onto the roads again, rocking and whining, lumber-
ing along at the pace of 1940 – thirty-five miles an hour, tops – their drivers looking small and nervous behind gauges that no longer work and
radiators spouting steam and steering wheels with too much play (but
wrapped in black electrician's tape for extra grip). The drivers look serious, caps pulled down over their eyes; it's harvest time, and the prices are
never right. But look at the grins on the faces of those trucks. On the
road again.

It's a chilly morning, and I'm down in my pond-side potting shed library, wrapped in a comforter. I've folded myself into a big brown vinyl
recliner that once belonged to my father's older brother, Herold, my
uncle Tubby.

It's as if this recliner were a bridge across the thirty years since he
died. And like a bridge, it creaks and sighs. When with a squeak its back
suddenly falls under my weight and its footrest throws my feet into the
air, I think of him, how he must have felt just as I feel. I see my shins
sticking out of my pant legs just as his did. His shins, white as alabaster,

were bald for a reason: "Armistice Day," he said. "It happened on Armistice Day in 1918. Your father and I were helping our cousin Ronald run the popcorn wagon. The streets were full of people celebrating, and everyone wanted a sack of popcorn. Ronald's popcorn wagon had a white gas-powered popper that sat down under the counter, and we kept it fired up until it was red-hot. It got so hot that all the hair on our legs fell out, and you know, it never grew back."

He was a lifelong bachelor who, like many work-centered men, died promptly upon his retirement, dismissing the rest of his life with a final shrug. He was borne across while sitting in this same recliner, his feet up before him, his leather bedroom slippers framing a small and ordinary section of the world.

He spent all of his working years in charge of the Visual Instruction Service at Iowa State College, where he quietly built what is today recognized as one of the country's most valuable collections of early industrial documentary films. His department loaned out and cared for all of the movie projectors and educational films that the college professors used in their classes, and the cool and quiet workrooms in which Uncle Tubby spent his days smelled of acetone and splicing glue.

In addition to the documentaries he collected, he had the foresight to purchase prints of many of the early animated cartoons, including an original "Steamboat Willie" that the college later sold back to Disney Studios for a great deal of money. He bought these films with us in mind, his nephew and niece, or so I think. When my sister and I were small and had regular birthday parties, he would set up a projector in my grandmother's backyard and show his collection of cartoons, using the side of her garage for a screen. This was in the 1940s – long before television reached our town – and animated cartoons were rare and wonderful. Our friends were envious of our luck in having an uncle who came furnished with movies.

This recliner sat in Uncle Tubby's office, and he sometimes inadvertently spent the night in it, having fallen asleep over a sheaf of correspondence or a copy of *Life* magazine. As he slept and snored, he was surrounded by miniature elephants that raised their trunks as if to trumpet back at him. He was an elephant collector and owned hundreds of them, big and small, glass and porcelain and carved from stone and ivory and wood. I have most of them now, and they stand along the top of a bookcase in our bedroom, facing the setting sun with the dust of the endless elephant roads on their backs.

Uncle Tubby was, of course, a kind of elephant himself, ponderous and solitary, so clumsy at his weight that one winter, when he'd dropped his car keys into a snowdrift, he snapped a twig from a nearby tree and poked it in the snow to mark the place till spring. He kept extra sets of keys for such emergencies. Like most large people, he radiated a good deal of moist heat. When I think of him, I immediately recall the pungent medicinal odor of red LifeBuoy soap and Old Spice cologne, a bracing and astringent combination.

His Methodist righteousness occasionally got the better of him, draining the color from his face. When he was angry, he drew in his cheeks and chewed on them, his eyes glittering with cold fire. The Koosers were never ones for displays of emotion, but I remember that in my presence he once walked up to a young couple who were having a loud argument on campus and shook the young man by the nape of the neck and told him he had no business speaking to a young lady in that fashion. Today he would have been booked for assault.

How sleepy a man can grow when he is full of memories. The book of autumn falls aside, and a breeze ruffles the illustrated pages of the leaves.

Early this morning I turned on our furnace for the first time. Though we have not yet had a frost, the chill of early autumn has come into the house, perhaps in the tattered carpetbags of the field mice moving into the cellar for winter. Falling leaves have begun to blow past the window, the lovely yellow leaves of time.

Kathleen and a half dozen friends, women in their late forties and early fifties, started tap dancing lessons last evening, and this morning, dressed in a businesslike brown suit and matching brown shoes, ready for a long day's work at the newspaper, she showed me four steps, tapping and shuffling and swinging her arms. I love this spirited woman to whom I've been married for more than twenty years, and I love the girl inside her. Shuffle-ball-change.

87

I've spent the past few days elbow to elbow with an old friend, Stewart, an artist who has bought an abandoned tavern in Valparaiso and is fixing it up for a painting studio and apartment. He plans to live in Nebraska a few months each year and spend the rest of the year in New York City, where he has lived and worked since the early seventies. We've been driving here and there in my pickup, hauling tools and supplies, a stove, a secondhand refrigerator. We were college friends in the sixties, a young poet and young painter, ready to take on the world, full of ourselves.

Yesterday, at a lumberyard in Lincoln, the clerk, a pretty young woman, looked us up and down with cool indifference and figured in the senior citizen's discount without asking our ages. It was quite a moment, two men still young in spirit at the turn of sixty years, with sunken eyes and wattles at the collar and fearsome medical histories, lugging a bright red plastic shop vac across the parking lot, laughing.

I'm back in Uncle Tubby's recliner this morning, a chilly breeze seeping in under the windows in my shed by the pond. With the footrest up, this chair is my magic carpet for flying into the past.

During the years when I was a child, the stores along Main Street were open on Saturday nights, and my uncle would load my enormous grandmother into the back seat of his black 1937 Ford and park it where she could watch the shoppers walk past. Everyone in Ames seemed to be on Main Street on Saturday night. My sister and I sometimes went along and would sit in the car with her, Judy in the back and I in front. Uncle Tubby would get out and walk off to visit with friends along the street. It was a boring way for a child to spend a couple of hours, sitting cooped up with an enormous old woman in a hot car, but there was a small hard rubber fan on the dashboard that fascinated me, and sometimes we'd see some of our friends walking past.

Grandmother always kept a scented handkerchief balled in her fist. When someone walked past with whom she wished to speak, she'd wave the handkerchief out the window and sweetly call "Yoo-hoo!" But when she saw someone she didn't like, and there were many who fit that description, she'd whisper gruffly to us, "There's that awful Mrs. Martin. Don't you children make a sound!"

88

She hadn't wanted her three sons to marry, but my father and my uncle Charlie had broken free. Despite the temptations he must surely have felt, my uncle Tubby stayed at my grandmother's side throughout her widowhood. They shared a rented house a few blocks from ours. She cooked, and he took care of the expenses. I remember a girlfriend he had for a time, a redhead named Harriet – fawn-colored suit, high heels, gloves, pillbox hat with a fawn-colored feather smoothed along the side. I suppose she gave up on him while he equivocated. By the time my grandmother died, Uncle Tubby was fifty years old, bald, overweight, and deeply set in his independent ways – too far gone in bachelorhood ever to free himself.

Grandmother Kooser died in 1949. She'd fallen and broken her shoulder, and because of her great weight, the bandages were so tight that they caused a blood clot that reached her heart. Despite the fact that she had disapproved of Father marrying Mother, she had been staying at our house since the fall, sleeping in my sister's bed and breaking it down in the middle so that it sagged with her impression for years afterward. My mother devotedly attended her. Although my memory is vague, I remember awakening on the morning of her death and wandering out in my pajamas to find the living room full of silent, dark-suited old men of her generation. They carried the faint odor of mothballs. This was a kind of solemnity of which I had never before been part.

Within the past week the leaves have begun to fall in earnest, and this morning the weatherman said it's possible we may have a little wet snow by morning. It's time to bring in the green tomatoes and wrap them in newspapers to ripen. And, among a hundred other fall chores, to clean the gutters along the roof. This past summer, one of my neighbors, standing in the drive, mentioned with a smile that I probably ought to get busy and clean them. Above our heads, a sunflower had sprouted, grown about two feet tall, and put out a tiny flower.

I drove to Lincoln yesterday on errands and spent a couple of hours in the public library leafing through a book of travel essays and observing the patrons. A library is like an airport; if you wait long enough, everybody in the world will walk past. And in a library there are a lot of people

89

who seem to be waiting for something like that to happen. The anticipation makes some of them very sleepy, and they nod off in their chairs, some of them peeing their pants.

There were a number of young people there to do research for school papers. They arrived in a noisy group and dispersed in hushed pairs. I heard a boy and girl ask the librarian to help them find the astrology section, and after they had located the book they were looking for, a big folio-sized book, they sat knee to knee on the floor and read it together.

For the past few years it's been fashionable for young women to wear ball caps and to snap the strap on the back under their ponytails. I like the looks of that, their shiny ponytails jauntily swinging, but it's hard not to think of the rear ends of horses. There's a piece of harness called the crupper that goes just under a horse's tail to keep its nose down. If the horse lifts its head to look for a way out of whatever predicament it's in, the crupper tightens and hurts the horse. But it's foolish for parents to think that a ball cap might keep a young woman from running away. Anybody can see they're made for running.

These young people toss their hair and glance about a lot, as if they were looking for mirrors. Theory has it that there was a time during the evolution of the human brain when people became aware of themselves. Before that, we grazed through the days like fat cattle. It never occurred to us to think of ourselves. The story of the tree of knowledge in the Garden of Eden may allude to that sudden awakening. If evolution is a continuing process of change and refinement, our self-awareness will also continue to evolve. Someday there may be mirrors everywhere you look.

❧

No fabulous treasure chest, hauled dripping in chains onto the deck of a ship, has ever spilled more pieces of gold than one locust tree in mid-October. My wife and I are just now overcome with riches, our front yard completely paved with tiny coins that, clinging to our feet, insinuate themselves into the house, the car, and even the secret, warm, grassy-smelling clefts in the paws of our dogs. Under the eaves, cobwebs strung by miserly spiders flutter with gold. Gold in the grass, gold falling from above, even little flurries of gold that lift from the grass and rise back into the air as if they weighed nothing, and, in fact, nothing they weigh. And all for free.

We have one fifty-foot locust in the front yard, accompanied by a half dozen offshoots, to use that word at its best. The locust has a bad reputation among landscapers, professional and amateur alike, because of its shoots, which disrupt those dreamed-of reaches of electric green, chemically enlightened grass. But I like to see the locust's offspring, a foot tall, defiantly waving their frondy little leaves. And I like the fierce look of the sharp black thorns and the ripply brown pods that dangle like strips of beef jerky from the full-grown trees.

Spring
Summer
Autumn
Winter

The eleventh edition of the *Encyclopedia Britannica*, published in 1917 and my favorite reference, says that the pods may be eaten by men and animals and that in Sicily a spirit is made from them. I know the effects of that spirit, a mild giddiness that comes while stumbling through a carpet of locust leaves on the way to the dark, tavernlike atmosphere of the outdoor toilet.

The Britannica says the husks are also called St John's bread, from a misunderstanding of Matt. 3:4, the passage in which John the Baptist is said to have lived on locusts and honey. But the locusts that John the Baptist ate to sustain himself in the desert were the kind with real wings, the kind that buzz going under the teeth, acceptable food in hard biblical times. Our locust leaves have a lust for riding the wind but never descend upon a field of wheat and eat it to the ground. A plague of falling locust leaves might ruin the looks of a golf course green, might annoy the president of a bank by blowing in under the door, but they do nothing else but make us rich with pleasure.

I suppose it's because autumn is a time of reflection, and because I've begun to spend so much time in this recliner, that my long-dead uncle is with me nearly every day.

After a front yard auction, at which he sold the furniture from my grandmother's rented house – I remember that two antique brass bedsteads sold for fifty cents each – Uncle Tubby moved into an apartment near the Iowa State College campus. It had two windows overlooking the top of a movie marquee. From those windows he could disapprove of the activities of the college students passing below.

He was at his office early and stayed late. During the week he often ate his evening meal at a restaurant out on the highway, sitting in the same booth if it was available and feeling put out if it was not. He often came to dinner at our house on Sundays and was always with us on holidays. He was a big eater. I liked to watch him drink from a glass because when he tipped his head back and closed his eyes, his throat trembled as if the flow of the water was a kind of silent warble. There was something wonderfully birdlike about it.

He had the loveliest whistle of anyone I've ever known. He could twitter and warble and flutter, the notes rising and falling, and then he would break off into beautiful, clear, sustained notes that pierced the air as he lumbered across campus, his hat pulled down square on his head. Blind Elmo Tanner on the radio was good at whistling, and the Hartz Mountain Canary show had cages full of canaries whistling along with the music they played, but neither show had a thing on my uncle Tubby, walking alone below the campus bell tower on a clear and starry night.

Stretching the patience of the university – its name had been changed from Iowa State College to Iowa State University by the time he grew old – he clung to his job past the usual retirement age, working until he was seventy. The university eventually had to hire three people to do the work he'd done. He moved his elephant collection and his big recliner into his apartment and settled in by the window over the movie house.

He was there for only a couple of months following his retirement. Comfortable new apartments had recently been built for college professors, and my parents and my uncle Charlie and aunt Dorothy encouraged him to move. It would be nice for him, they said, to have a fresh new place. He had by then lived in his old apartment for more than twenty years, and it was like a second skin. The smell of LifeBuoy had seeped into the woodwork, and everything had taken on the same dark colors of his businesslike clothes. The university's successful pressure on him to retire had accustomed him to giving in, and he reluctantly agreed to take one of the new apartments.

On the morning he was to move, the moving men climbed the stairs to find the door ajar and my uncle dead in his recliner. He had politely unbolted the door to wait for them, sat back in his recliner, and his heart had stopped. There was an antacid tablet in his mouth. It may have been that he had been treating heart pain with Tums for many years.

On a stand near his recliner was a big book on the lives of elephants, filled with color photographs. When my uncle Charlie and I went through his belongings later, I opened this book to where it had been marked with a slip of paper. The marked section was about the deaths of elephants. It described how elephants lie down by the road each night to sleep and how in the morning some of the old ones find it difficult to rise to their feet and go on and how the young ones encourage them by butting them with their heads. But sometimes the old ones do not have the will or strength to rise, and the herd moves on without them, leaving them to die. Just as my uncle died, there, by the side of the road, urged to move on but not able to.

It's a very comfortable resting place, this old recliner, and sometimes I fall asleep while reading in it. I awaken from my dreams looking out between my feet at the pond and the hill beyond it, the seasons changing, my breath before me floating on the air. But it's a chair with a mind of its own. When you want to get out, it subtly resists; its hinges and braces stick just a little. You must heave your weight forward to get the footrest to drop so that you can unfold and roll out. Once out, you feel stiff and heavy on your feet, a little lightheaded too, from sleeping there. It is a chair that, if it could, would hold you in its fat brown arms forever.

Because we've had a forecast of rain, the farmers were in the fields until late last night, combines roaring, their headlights illuminating rolling clouds of pale yellow dust. Above them was a sliver of moon, vague behind thin clouds briskly blowing east.

I have always been enchanted by lights like those – pinpoints of farmyard lights against the ten o'clock darkness of rural America, headlights of farm machinery crawling over the fields, lonely street lamps in villages illuminating empty intersections.

The Joslyn Museum in Omaha owns a 1948 painting by George Ault called *August Night at Russell's Corners*, portraying two old buildings and a section of road illuminated by a single hanging light. One side of a red building to the left is lighted, one side of a red building to the right. The

93

road curves slightly, as indicated by a painted centerline, and abruptly vanishes into the darkness. Recently, I was asked to submit a poem about a favorite picture for a book planned by the Harry Abrams Company, and I chose this painting. It seems to have a simple premise: old buildings that in daylight would be so familiar that a person living in Russell's Corners wouldn't even notice them become exotic and mysterious in the light from a commonplace bulb. Ault made four paintings of this same midnight crossroads, each from a slightly different angle, some showing a third building. But their effect upon me is identical. I can feel my will joining with that of the feeble light in its struggle to push back the darkness, darkness that has already begun to affect and alter the familiar, making it strange and exciting. I wrote:

Spring
Summer
Autumn
Winter

If you can awaken
inside the familiar
and discover it new
you need never
leave home.

Local wonders.

❧

If this small, colorful windfall apple were an art nouveau painted glass lampshade from the years just before the Great War, and if my Grandmother Kooser, then in her thirties, were to enter her shadowy parlor, wearing a shawl against the cold, and come near and bend to turn up the wick, my hands, which cup the apple and which in my imagination are becoming the walls of that room, would glow red and green and oil lamp yellow, and there would be dark patches here and there, like leaves, from the apple's spots of mildew, and a blur of coppery brown on one wall where the apple had lain against something and bruised its skin. And on this breezy autumn afternoon, with apples thudding onto the grass beyond the window, if she were to place her hands on this painted shade to warm them and then were to sigh and turn away and enter a darker room, I would be left like this, alone at the end of an instant in which my grandmother returned to place an apple in my hands and then was gone.

❧

94

It's a rainy morning, and I've forsaken the Bohemian Alps to take care of a family errand in Iowa. I'm driving east along a section of the old Lincoln Highway across Marshall County. You know this road, or one just like it – a narrow winding ribbon of concrete, broken up like river ice by some fifty-odd winters of heaving frost and patched in a thousand places by velvety black asphalt that turns so soft in July and August you can pinch up a wad and chew it like Blackjack gum. The tires slap along over the mended seams with the same easy rhythm set up by the wiper blades. A yellow maple leaf the size of a child's hand presses itself to a corner of the windshield.

Spring

Summer

Autumn

Winter

What used to be U.S. Highway 30 is now, officially, an unnumbered road in the care of the county. Highway 30 is now a new divided four lane a couple miles south. The highway is like a dry wash left by a river that's changed its channel, like a bullsnake skin, spotted black and gray, cast off in the woods to dry up and blow away. Once a week, a county maintenance man drives a yellow pickup slowly along its length, gazing into the ditch as if he were checking his trotlines and hoping that nothing was on them.

Things close in on an old road, but it still knows its way out. Pressing against it and reaching out over it are groves of oak and maple and hickory and box elder. Buckbrush and burrs move up out of the ditches. Grasses bend over it, blurring its edges. But the Lincoln Highway pushes on, like a silver streamliner out of the forties, racing past clusters of fading signs that lean this way and that, reminiscing about long-lost motels and forgotten brands of motor oil.

I pass through State Center, "The Rose Capitol of Iowa." The red of the roses is gone with the summer. Today is a day for a particular yellow, the yellow of a washtub of marigolds in front of a bungalow; the yellow of a school bus – parked and ticking under a dripping tree – its hood still warm beneath red leaves that have just now fallen there; the yellow of SLOW CHILDREN signs. (Inside the school, at their little desks, sit the slow children.)

Taped to the windows of the schoolrooms and to the windows of little clapboard houses along the highway are orange paper jack-o'-lanterns, black cats with raised tails and fiery orange eyes, white skeletons with little silver rivets joining their awkward bones. In front of one old house is a shock of corn, sagging in the rain as if it were made of papier-mâché. A fat pumpkin nestles into its weary skirts.

Spring
Summer
Autumn
Winter

The windows of many of these houses are warm with the sort of yellow light that fills small kitchens with wooden cupboards that have been painted a hundred times, kitchens with old linoleum turning up along the baseboards, kitchens in which the coffee is on, in which the white porcelain sink is never completely dry to the touch, in which a woman of indefinite age is wiping her hands on her apron or pushing her hair back from her face with her fingertips or holding her hands out before her and looking down upon their veiny backs with mild wonder, as if they were old newspapers she'd just found lying under the honeysuckle bushes. Daydream believer, homecoming queen.

This is the life I have chosen, one in which I can pass by on the outside, looking back in – into a world in static diorama, the world that Edward Hopper seemed to see. Driving east, the globe spins beneath me, the marigold yellow centerline on the old Lincoln Highway like a stripe on a whistling top. State Center rushes into the past, bright yellow leaves flying behind.

❧

There are a lot more Halloween decorations on houses in Lincoln and in the surrounding towns than I remember people having in previous years. Even orange icicles! A couple of years ago strings of electrically illuminated plastic icicles were introduced as new Christmas decorations. People festooned them from their eaves. Unlike real icicles, they had staggered branches like little bolts of lightning, but apparently they were successful even though they didn't look much like real icicles, so successful the manufacturers have apparently decided to mix orange dye into the molds, hoping to pick up a little Halloween business. Once again we have carried things a little too far.

Stewart phoned at 5:30 this morning asking if I'd drive to Lincoln to jump-start his 1968 Cadillac. He'd taken it to a car wash and sprayed the carburetor with water, and he'd run the battery down trying to start it. He owns an old Buick that he drove here from New York and an old pickup and old Cadillac he's bought since arriving here. During the past couple of weeks we've had to tow, push, jumpstart, and then give up on each of them once if not twice.

He told me to meet him at a nearby pancake house. This particular pancake house is open at all hours and is favored by recovering alcoholics, who meet there to drink coffee, smoke, and talk, and the management is used to eccentric behavior. There sat Stewart in his Halloween costume, a white paper suit, a long curly black wig, and a red plaid hunting cap with the earflaps down. In the shadows of the wig was his grinning face. We had pancakes before driving my jeep to the car wash. A woman dressed as a Christmas tree came over and stood by our booth and encouraged us to attend an AA meeting. She looked closely at Stewart's black wig and asked if he was an Indian.

The Cadillac wouldn't start.

Pheasant season starts tomorrow, and on the next few weekends, dozens of pickups will be meandering from side to side down our road, their drivers and passengers peering out into the cornfields from under the bills of their orange caps, not paying the slightest attention to where they're going. Guns don't kill people, people driving pickups kill people. Road hunting, which is what these fellows are up to, amounts to suddenly yelling with glee, slamming on the brakes, flinging the doors wide, jumping out both sides of the truck, and blasting away at some unfortunate pheasant that only wanted to pick up a few grains of the county's road gravel. This style of hunting is against the law – against a half dozen laws, I'd guess – but we Seward County taxpayers refuse to pay for the use of excessive force. After all, we rarely need to call in the law, living in an area where the most egregious offense is borrowing a tool and not returning it. People don't lock the doors to their houses, and the only reason they lock their cars is, in August, to keep neighbors from putting zucchini in the back seat. The last time I saw the sheriff on our road was several years ago when a farm boy who'd lost his girlfriend set fire to a couple of hay bales out of frustration. First came the convoy of pickups that make up the volunteer fire department, then the sheriff's big white-and-gold cruiser roared by, trailing a cloud of dust, lights flashing and siren screaming. Our hens didn't lay any eggs for a week. So, if you must go out onto the roads during pheasant season, it pays to keep far over to the right side. Just over the crown of the next hill, you could suddenly come upon a pickup worth a lot more than your house, with four-wheel drive to boot, abandoned right in the middle of the road, with two or three strangers in orange vests in pursuit of a pheasant, stumbling along in the ditch like a lost survey crew.

One morning during last year's pheasant season, I stopped in the Cornhusker Hotel in Lincoln to use their toilet. It's gotten almost impossible to find a restroom anywhere in town, and I can't tell you why. I find myself looking for toilets more and more frequently the older I get, but I gather that everyone else must be getting the call less and less. Anyway, in the lobby of the hotel, I came upon a couple of young pheasant hunters with starched and pressed Desert Storm camouflage outfits and brand-new phosphorescent caps and vests. They looked like recently graduated chiropractors, with that air of righteous certainty about them, as if all of the problems in the world could be solved by a series of spinal adjustments. One was on each end of a big green Coleman cooler, and they were lugging it toward the door through the traveling salesmen. Pheasant hunting can consume a lot of beer, and these two were ready for a day of trying work. Having gotten a good look at them, I kept close to the house once I got home.

I hunted when I was younger, but after I moved to the country, I swore off making loud noises except in the case of emergencies. When a gun goes off, it alters everything in the immediate vicinity, and this effect lasts for a good half hour. Every sparrow, every field mouse, every spider in its web freezes in place. Shooting guns and setting off Fourth of July firecrackers are far too much of an imposition on the natural world. None of our fellow creatures has evolved far enough to accept guns or loud noises as part of the order of things. These days I only use my shotgun for occasional tree trimming. An adjustable choke twelve-gauge pump is perfect for knocking down objectionable branches that you can't reach with a ladder. If a fellow's a decent shot, he can take off a limb two inches thick with a half box of number six shells. I prefer rabbit and squirrel load for pruning, but pheasant load will do in a pinch. I keep a single-shot twenty-gauge for the lighter branches.

My neighbor across the road has a state-licensed shooting preserve he's named CAN HUNT. Its logo is a tin can with the lid pried up and a couple of pheasants flying out of it. For a fee, you can shoot pheasants and partridges that he raises in pens and will hide here and there in his fields and pastures. It's sort of like hunting. You can drive out from Lincoln or Omaha in your new sports utility vehicle, wearing your Cabela's hunting outfit, and spend a few hours with your friends and your bird dogs, who don't know the difference between a pen-raised pheasant and a wild one.

Some Saturdays there are a dozen vehicles parked near CAN HUNT headquarters, a pair of corn cribs dragged up together and cobbled into a building where on bad days you can get in out of the rain.

I noticed last week that there's a new sign on the headquarters building: ORGANICHUNTING.COM, and I punched it up on the Internet and took a look at the photographs of pretty much the same hunters and dogs I can some days see right on the other side of the road.

A few days after a CAN HUNT canned hunt, a pen-raised pheasant that has miraculously escaped the hunters and dogs can be seen standing dazed on the gravel road, so tame it doesn't know about people and won't get out of the way. The mail carrier has to swerve to get around it. We had one with its tail shot off that came to our birdfeeder last winter, a colorful giant among the drab juncos and sparrows. It stayed around till its tail feathers grew back, and then it walked on.

While I was writing this afternoon, I became aware of a light tapping at the window, which is on the north side of the house. I got up to look and discovered that dozens of ladybugs (or ladybirds, as some call them) were flying into the window, bumping against the glass, and falling away. What were they up to? Is it possible they migrate? They seem so clumsy and slow, with wings no bigger than nail parings. How can they possibly fly far enough south to escape cold weather? Especially with houses standing in the way. How enormous an obstacle a house must be to a tiny creature like that!

And though lots of creatures are restless and moving on, some settle in. I picked up a pine cone that fell just yesterday, and some tiny creature had already built a tight warm cocoon between two of its vacant seed chambers.

Spring
Summer
Autumn
Winter

Earlier in the day, feeling vaguely restless myself, I drove west on gravel roads through the village of Staplehurst and on to Thayer, a sad little crossroads with not much life left in it. There's an elevator there, and a couple of men were augering grain into storage bins, but the rest of the town was empty. The Thayer Bank, once a smart brick building with white stone trim, is just a shell. You can look through the broken-out front window and see the weeds behind the building because the rear wall has collapsed. Across the street from the bank is the only other business building still standing, a tavern with dust-covered windows, one window upstairs broken out or fallen out. Just north of the tavern is a little park with a dozen horseshoe pits, the grass unmowed and strewn with leaves, the stakes rusty. Like a ladybug, I had bumped up against the north side of something that seemed to me to have enormous presence, an empty building once full of music and laughter and the smells of smoke and beer and polish sausage and pickled eggs. You can't forget the pickled eggs, especially if you're getting ready to set out on a long trip into the future.

It's a pleasantly warm day for my wife's birthday, and she's driven off to work wearing the amethyst ring I gave her.

Since her departure I've been getting dirty straightening up the barn. Lots of people who live in the country have a capacity for hoarding, and I am among them. I find it difficult to throw away anything, believing that this little scrap of wire or this four-foot section of garden hose might come in handy for something someday. It's ten miles to the nearest hardware store, and besides, the prices keep going up and up. The box of brass pipe fittings I bought for a couple of dollars at a sale in Ulysses a couple of years ago would cost close to a hundred dollars to replace. I never seem to need brass fittings, but there's something to be said for having a box available, just in case.

Like a lot of other hoarders, I've gone to yard sales and purchased jars of miscellaneous screws, cardboard boxes full of odd plumbing fittings, buckets of turnbuckles and small wheels and old pulleys and scraps of chain. It is so difficult to throw out anything that my autumn barn straightening is just that, a reordering of my hoard, though I did manage to fill a box with things I've kept for ten or fifteen years and never found a use for: some rusted wire window screens, a few short pieces of electrical wire, a couple of dried-up cans of paint.

When Stewart started fixing up his old building, he came down several times and browsed through the barn. I was able to give him all sorts of items he needed: lengths of lumber, some galvanized heating ducts, a couple of windows, and two big skylights. He was most appreciative and remarked that my barn offers "convenient one-stop shopping."

You find things, and you keep them. Yesterday Kathleen and I walked a mile of dirt road, up and back, picking up litter. This morning, when I was getting ready for my daily walk, I discovered that one of my leather gloves was missing. I thought that perhaps I'd dropped it on yesterday's walk and decided to drive back over there and walk the same mile to see if I could find it. That road is little traveled, and there was a chance that the glove might be lying there undisturbed.

As I approached the far end of the mile, two pheasant hunters in a Jeep Cherokee passed me, went to the next crossroads, and came back. The driver stopped beside me and rolled down the window. "Need any help?" he asked.

"No," I said, "I'm just out for a walk. I sometimes walk this mile and pick up trash."

"Did you lose a glove yesterday?" he asked.

"I sure did," I said, "I've been looking for it."

"I've got it in the back seat here. I thought it might get ruined if it rained."

How fine I look this morning in my new plaid flannel shirt from the Junior League Thrift Shop in Lincoln! Blues and reds and greens. I bought it yesterday for five bucks, twice what I'd pay at other thrift shops, but I don't mind paying a little extra for the old shirts of doctors and lawyers, whose spouses are Junior Leaguers. The clothes are of the best quality and carry the best labels. This shirt cost its owner around forty dollars, I figure, and it was only worn a few times. That lack of wear probably means it *didn't* cost its owner forty dollars but cost its owner's *wife* forty dollars when she bought it for him as a gift, thinking he might like to look a little countrified when he went to the tailgate party before the football game. But he didn't wear it more than a few times, dutifully, and then he went right back to his red running outfit with the white stripe down the legs. So she gave this fine shirt to the Junior League Thrift Shop, and now it's mine. The label says "Legend," an appropriate brand for a man who likes stories.

❧

I took a break from raking leaves and started to go through a box of things I brought back from Mother's house in Iowa. When my parents moved into their new house, in Ames, Iowa, in 1953, they started keeping a guest book, and this morning I came upon it. It's the sort of thing you'd buy in a card and gift shop, with an artificial leather binding overstamped with fleur-de-lis. Inside, on lines set out for GUESTS, are about 150 signatures and addresses, entered during the next nine years and culminating in 1962 when my parents moved away from their wide circle of friends in Ames and took up residence in Cedar Rapids, where for the next few years they knew few people and had few visitors.

But here they all were, the signatures of people who made up the adult backdrop for my childhood. The first names, carefully written on the first line of the first page, are those of my great aunt Carrie Lang and her daughter Lucille. Aunt Carrie was married to my Grandmother Kooser's only brother, Frank, and she worked at home, baking pies and cakes for the Sheldon Munn Hotel. Uncle Frank, who was a veteran of the Great War, stayed at home. Lucille, one of two daughters, had studied piano and aspired to be a concert performer. She married a man who had an oil distributorship in Iowa City, and after she was married for a few years, she gave up the piano and, as my parents' generation said, took to drink. Father and Mother visited them one afternoon, and Lucille's husband entertained them in the living room, serving cookies and iced tea. Lucille was somewhere in the house but didn't appear.

On the next line is Arnold Livingston, my father's best friend, who traveled to Yellowstone Park with my father when they were young men. Somewhere among my keepsakes is a snapshot of them standing in knickers, blousy shirts, and floppy snap-brim hats beside the Packard touring car they drove. Arnold died in his fifties of a heart attack. My family would have used the term "massive heart attack." I never heard a heart attack described in any other way.

Spring
Summer
Autumn
Winter

His wife, Margaret, who signed after her husband, was a big woman who moved as if she were a piano rolling on casters. She had narcolepsy and couldn't keep from dropping into a deep sleep at inappropriate moments. Arnold would jab her in the ribs to wake her. She did what she could to disguise her problem, saying she'd had a sleepless night, and so on. After she'd been widowed, my father and mother, one spring day, took her to a park to look at the flowers. She loved flowers and knew a great deal about them. She fell asleep at the end of a bench, tilted precariously over the end, her chin down as if she were looking at something on the ground. In a few moments she woke and, without changing the position of her head, said, "Oh, look! A little Queen Anne's lace!"

After my parents moved to Cedar Rapids, I roomed with Margaret for my last semester of college. She sometimes fell asleep in the bathtub. The bathroom was adjacent to my room, and I would hear her splashing about as she bathed. Then, suddenly, a vast silence would descend. I would sit there helpless, knowing that she'd nodded off and fearing that she might slip under the water and drown. At the same time, I was afraid to open the door and embarrass her. The silence would last ten or fifteen minutes, until the water cooled enough to wake her. Then I'd hear splashing as she got out of the tub, and I could breathe again.

Her house was always a mess, not dirty but cluttered. She couldn't throw away a thing. Newspapers, magazines, catalogs, correspondence, books. She had some wonderful old scrapbooks kept by her father, filled with clippings of popular verse from the annual meetings of the Grand Army of the Republic. She had boxes of old photographs, boxes of old hats and scarves and dresses. Arnold's clothes hung in a closet years after his death. Only the front door could be used because the back stair was completely blocked with cartons of keepsakes. She kept the door to her bedroom closed because it was stacked almost to the ceiling.

When she was young and single, she'd been head dietician for the Cook County Hospital in Chicago, and she was a marvelous cook. Only one burner on the stove was clear of dishes, pots, and pans, but she cooked wonderful meals in one small skillet. Somehow she could manage a course of meat, a course of vegetables, and a course of potatoes in one nine-inch skillet. We ate our evening dinner from two tiny cleared places on the dining room table, talking together around and over the stacks of things piled between us. She often fell asleep during a meal, and I would sit back and wait to start eating again until she'd awakened, so she wouldn't feel that she'd missed out on something.

Spring

Summer

Autumn

Winter

I plan to keep this old guest book on my desk and look at it from time to time. Marcel Proust had the taste of a biscuit to take him back through time, and I have this.

❧

Sumac. It's a beautiful plant in autumn, spatters of apple red in the ditches and fencerows. Most of the locals call it buckbrush because their fathers and grandfathers called it that (my own grandfather called it *shoe-mack*, but he was an eccentric who also called asparagus *sparrow grass*), but somebody, years ago, must have seen the shapes of antlers in its branches and nudged the metaphor along just far enough to get it rolling. It wasn't that he was an especially compelling talker, but once the connection to antlers was made, a lot of other people began to see them too. A good metaphor is like that; it changes the way you look at the world. But the people who live near me have adjusted it just a little. Buckbrush was once called staghorn sumac, but if you said something about a stag around here, you'd get a funny look, and there's nothing much worse than a funny look when you live in a small town. Nobody talks about stags. That's like talking about swine. You leave swine to the bankers and ag professors. To fit in around here, you talk about bucks and pigs, or bucks and hogs.

❧

At a welding shop: Four slat-backed chairs pushed up around a table make a big basket. Fill it up once with smoky light and men in overalls and the hot rustle of pinochle cards, and you have harvested enough for any rainy Friday.

❧

What is it the wind has lost that it keeps looking under every leaf this way? All day I've watched her angrily pacing, muttering under her breath. She is going to be late, I suppose, for some important engagement. She is saying, I think, that she set it down only a moment ago, whatever it was, and now it has vanished, along with a necklace of geese and the icy lingerie of rain.

🍂

Stewart and I drove to Dwight for lunch at Cy's. There are only a handful of businesses in Dwight – Cy's, two taverns that also serve lunch, a barbershop, a laundromat, a few other miscellaneous businesses. Cy's burned down after Cy died, and his wife built a new Cy's on the same lot. They make fresh cake doughnuts on Sundays, but it wasn't Sunday, so we asked about the daily special – roast pork, dressing, sweet kraut, potatoes with gravy, and a piece of light rye bread. That's too much food for me, I told the waitress, a pleasant plump woman with three colored rhinestones in the rim of her ear and a red sweatshirt. "We've got small," she said, so we both ordered the small. Three-fifty for a big plateful. It wasn't really the small but the regular, priced down to a small for us.

A friend recently told me that there's an Italian restaurant in Bakersfield, California, where the waitresses give you a neck rub while you're ordering. "It's not erotic," she said. "They're all fifty- and sixty-year-old women. That's just what they do there." You'd get in a lot of trouble at Cy's if you asked for a neck rub.

A broadly smiling woman with twinkling spectacles came in and sat at the next table. She was in her fifties, wearing a man's tan wool snap-brim hat and a makeshift serape that appeared to be an embroidered dresser scarf with a neck hole. She was talking to a man at her table but talking to everyone else in the room as well, her voice as wide as her smile. Soon she began to talk directly to us and got up and stood at the end of our table and asked for our names and where we lived and pointed to a blue pheasant embroidered on the front of her serape and said it commemorated her mother. Then she said she was an orphan and didn't know much about her mother. Stewart and I kept forking in our roast pork and kraut, and she kept talking. She said her husband has worked at a plant in Lincoln for twenty-two years and she spends her days driving handicapped people on their errands. She said they call her the orphan lady because she takes up with lonely people because she

105

is an orphan and sympathizes with them. She said they call her the hat lady because she likes to wear peculiar hats. It seemed to me that the important part of what she was telling us was the "they call me" part, as if it were important to her that "they" were calling her something.

Stewart lives most of the year in New York City, where there is an abundance of people like the orphan lady and the hat lady. In Dwight, Nebraska, one hat lady has to stand for a lot of people. Maybe that's the point of being called the hat lady and the orphan lady and whatever else they may call her. It makes her seem like many people, and she is speaking for them all.

After we left Cy's, we walked a couple of blocks through bright sunshine, clear autumn air, and falling leaves to the grounds of the Catholic church. I wanted to show Stewart a tiny chapel there, one of the wonders of the Bohemian Alps.

The chapel sits in the shade of the church, a yellow brick cathedral with a spire and exterior buttressing. The chapel is wooden, painted brown, about ten feet by ten feet, with a sharply gabled roof. Inside, the light is thin and lightly washed with gold. The windows are small and let in very little light. There are two kneeling benches, a box for alms, and a high altar with an icon of Christ painted in black on brass.

When your eyes adjust, you see her. Below the altar is a glass case like an oversized aquarium, and in it is a life-sized dummy of a young woman with a gash in the side of her neck. She has long brown hair – real human hair, donated by a girl from Dwight, many years ago – and she lies on her right side with the hair spilling over her face. Her white hands, made of that kind of material you associate with department store manikins, are extended beyond her blue robe, and she holds out the index and ring fingers of one hand, a sign of Christian faith.

St. Cecelia, saint of music, who was killed for trying to protect some Christians from the Romans. The Romans first tried to smother her by blocking off her chimney, then broke in and killed her with an axe. And here she lies, in Dwight, Nebraska, in near darkness, without a funny hat.

These late-fall, early-winter days are sometimes so still and sunny that they look like painted backdrops. And this morning, against such a backdrop, sitting in my uncle's recliner, I have been remembering being a little boy during World War II.

I was born in the spring of 1939, when, far beyond the serrated corn-field horizons of Iowa, Eastern Europe was tooth and claw at war. Ames was a peaceable, elm-shaded town, dead center in the continent, and though it would eventually be proven that our fifteen thousand citizens had always been safe from the Axis Powers, we weren't to relax until peace was declared. Though we were never to hear the searing whistles of v-2 rockets or feel the ground-shuddering thumps of falling block-busters or smell any smoke other than that of our own leaf fires on peaceful October evenings, we had been warned that there was always the possibility we might be attacked from the air by long-range German bombers, and we watched the skies, ready to huddle under the basement stairs when we heard the roar of the Luftwaffe and the blitz came hur-tling down.

As the war grew and took America in, I began to grow up among adults descended from immigrants. Although I was much too young to understand it as a boy, this pioneer background influenced the way the older generation behaved. My parents and their neighbors had learned from their forebears to prepare for the worst. A Nazi air attack was just one of many horrible things that might happen to a family along the long, hard, Calvinistic trail to life's end. But years before, in the dark for-ests of Europe, our ancestors had developed a charm against ill fortune such as we now faced. It was what today's therapists refer to as magical thinking.

For example, when my family prepared to embark upon an excursion, my mother, like her mother and, I suppose, her grandmother and great grandmother before her, would pause on the front stoop while the rest of us waited in the idling car. Gripping her purse in both hands and blankly staring into the middle distance, she would silently go over all of the awful things that might befall us: (1) we might have a flat tire, and if we did, (2) you never knew who might come along and try to take ad-vantage of you there by the side of the road, or (3) a truck might come along and blow the car off the jack and hurt one of us, and (4) where could medical help be found for someone badly injured, perhaps bleed-

107

ing to death, there by the road? And so on, down the long bitter litany of potential misfortunes. By listing all those possible horrors, you somehow kept them from happening. "You never know" became a kind of motto, and it could be tailored to the fear of bombing raids.

So the people of Ames, locked in a common dread of the possible, stood frozen on their front stoops, staring into space, silently preparing for an attack by the Germans from one direction or the Japanese from the other. You never knew if the camouflaged bombers might be approaching, hidden from view amidst the shining cottonwood fluff that spiraled high over the fields on summer thermals. Though it was reported that German and Japanese submarines had been sighted off the coasts, the danger never came any closer than that. A childhood friend told me recently that he always felt secure during those years because he was certain President Roosevelt lived just up the street from our house, at Roosevelt Elementary School. In fact, he said, he had been told that Sir Winston Churchill had visited the president there.

Spring

Summer

Autumn

Winter

Helen Molleston has died at 92. There was a letter in my box this morning.

She was the last living friend and neighbor of my parents. In one of her journals, May Sarton says something to the effect that one of the saddest days of her life was when she realized that there was no one still living who remembered what she had been like as a child.

On my desk among all the other odds and ends I've collected is a wooden potato masher that Helen gave me twenty years ago. It is turned from maple and shaped – how is it shaped? – if you spun a cleaver on the axis of the back of its blade, it would make that shape. It came from the First Methodist Church in Ames, Iowa, my family's church and the church where Helen, a tall woman of plain tastes, soberly sang in the choir. Among those plain tastes were those for church suppers with mashed potatoes. How much I will miss this woman, the last to die of my parent's generation and therefore the one who, without ever knowing it, has carried the burden of being my last living link to their time.

Kathleen and I have been forced by good sense to discontinue our early morning walks for the duration of this week. It's the weeklong season for hunting deer with rifles, and it's dangerous to be out walking the roads without wearing bright colors. And no colors, even those Day-Glo oranges, are bright colors before the sun comes up. We'll have to watch the Leonid meteor shower from our own yard, God's own tracer rounds streaking across the heavens.

🌿

The coyotes have been crying these past few mornings at three or four, up on the hill behind our house. If you've never heard coyotes, their cry is as wild and hysterical a barking and yipping as you could imagine. Sounds like theirs must have come out of the narrow windows of castles during the inquisition. A cousin of mine who lives in the east, a composer of music, was out here a few years ago and couldn't get enough of listening to them. I've been expecting to hear their cries in one of his recordings.

The past few weeks, I've been seeing coyote hunters during the day with their jeeps and pickups parked by the road, talking into walkie-talkies, dead-serious looks on their faces. In their camouflage clothes, they look like members of a SWAT team about to break into a methamphetamine lab. They must imagine that there's some danger. Are the coyotes armed and dangerous?

The procedure is to post hunters on all four sides of a section of land and then to try to frighten the coyote into running within rifle range of one of the men on the periphery. Once you've shot a coyote or two, you're done for the day and can go get a pizza.

Coyotes eat mice and grasshoppers and rabbits, when they can catch them. They especially love mice, and I've seen them playfully tossing mice in the air. It's said they'll kill pets and team up on a calf that's gotten separated from its mother, but to my knowledge, that's mostly hunters' lore. There are plenty of rabbits, mice, and grasshoppers. Coyote hunting can't be justified on the basis of the damage they do. Shooting coyotes is really just fun, a man with a high-powered rifle trying to see if he can hit and kill a frightened creature that can't shoot back.

Coyote hunters say that there will always be plenty of coyotes, that there are too many of them to ever be completely eradicated. Maybe that's true; coyotes are clever. But I don't like the thought of their being driven so far back into the wilderness that we won't be able to hear them crying in the early morning.

Spring

Summer

Autumn

Winter

☙

Now that we've set aside daylight saving time, it gets dark very early. The world beyond the windows is black by six o'clock.

We had frequent blackouts during the war years, and as my family sat in our darkened bungalow, we could hear the stealthy tread of our fat, moon-faced neighbor, Mr. Posey, as he passed. He was our neighborhood's civil defense observer, and it was his duty to see if any light showed beneath drawn blinds. If he saw any, he would rap sharply on the glass with a short black stick, and the lights inside the chastened house would immediately snap out, as if by magic.

Sometimes I hid behind the Mezvinskys' honeysuckle hedge and watched Mr. Posey waddle past, wearing his Frank Buck white pith helmet that glowed like a lampshade. That spot of white must have presented the only visible bombing target in the darkened town. He was one of those fat men who could move as gracefully as a ballerina, as if he were on silent rollers, and he would emerge from the darkness, float past, and vanish, his Old Spice after-shave perfuming the darkness.

My uncle Tubby was a civil air observer. It was his responsibility to identify the silhouettes of incoming bombers against the sky. The Civil Air Patrol had assigned him a set of hard rubber models of enemy aircraft, wonderfully detailed, to hold over his head and study. I was not permitted to play with them, but I coveted them from a distance. For years I have searched flea markets and antique shops hoping to find just one of these magnificent models, but they have all been rolled into the dark deep hangar of the past.

The Atomic Energy Commission had a laboratory at Iowa State College in Ames, including a mysterious cyclotron that whirled round and round in a low brick building behind a chain-link fence in the woods. I have since learned that the blackouts were intended in part to protect that building and the secret work being done there. Something the engineers and physicists were doing there was connected with the Manhattan Project. When I was a little older, after the war, my friends and I used to hang on the fence trying to see what was going on, absorbing all

manner of radiation, I suppose. (That, in addition to the radiation I got
by sticking my feet in the x-ray machine in the shoe department of my
father's store.)

Spring

Summer

Autumn

Winter

Wheat and oats are grasses. Corn too is a grass. Once you understand
that, you begin to see how Great Plains agriculture works. Generations
of farmers have made their living by growing grass in a grassy place.
What gets in the way of the grasses living out their own sweet lives, as
they have for eons, is the farmer, who has to extract enough extra from
the grass to be able to feed himself, his hogs and cattle, and the rest of us.
That's where the trouble starts. The culture of the Great Plains is everywhere shaded by the trouble of trying to get the grass to give enough.

Our grain farmers had an enormous harvest this fall – mountains of
corn and milo heaping up next to the elevators, poured out by augers
that, with their long necks, look a little like brontosaurs. But the crop's
too good to be worth much. That's farming: huge surpluses of grain one
year, with low prices because of the abundance; then, the following year,
a poor crop resulting in higher prices per bushel. And so it goes, year in
and year out, supply and demand, demand and supply. Nearly every person who farms in our area has a day job in Seward or Lincoln and farms
in the evenings and on weekends. But it's still a good life. "Not even a
chicken digs for nothing."

Many of the Bohemians who came to this country had lived and worked
in cities. They were tradespeople, actors, bankers, musicians. They had
to learn farming. They arrived in their wool suits and good dresses and
had to get dirty to live. One of Willa Cather's Czech characters, Mr.
Shimerda, a violinist, kills himself because he can't adjust to the empty
open spaces of Nebraska.

Saline County, a little south of the Bohemian Alps, was also settled by
Czechs and at one time was said to have America's highest per capita suicide rate. I asked a historian to explain this, and he said that he suspected
it was because a number of the Czechs were freethinkers. Without faith
to turn to, they couldn't fight off the despair when they found themselves alone and unappreciated on the desolate plains.

I've been thinking about poor Mr. Shimerda this morning and about his violin and about how he was buried at a crossroads. The Czechs believed that the spirits of suicides were restless and could only be kept in their graves if they had a cross laid over them. Many of the graves in Czech cemeteries are covered by full-length stone slabs, and some of these have crosses on them. But surely not all of those people were suicides.

The violin player, Mr. Shimerda, fell apart when he felt himself alone, and my friend, Dave Fowler, has written about how violins fall apart when they are left unplayed. Here's some of what Dave has told me:

Spring
Summer
Autumn
Winter

Assume the violin is still in tune and the bow is loosened when it's put back into its case. For some reason, the owner does not return. The case with the fiddle may be moved to a spare room, then to the basement, then to the attic. Many of the old cases were wooden "coffin" cases, affording less protection to the instrument and adding to the rattle that increases as parts come loose.

First, the tuning pegs will start to slip, and the strings will loosen or go completely slack. In time, a gut-type string will dry out and break. The pegs may slip out of their holes and roll around in the case.

Next, once the strings are loose, the bridge will fall over. The tailpiece, looped over a button at the bottom of the violin, will then slip off the violin.

Next, the sound post falls over. The sound post is a small Tinkertoy-like dowel that sits inside the violin just under the bridge and transfers vibration from the top of the instrument to the back. With less pressure from the strings to hold it in place, the stick will fall over, rattling about when the instrument is moved.

If a tightened bow is left in the case, it may warp. Tight or loose, the bow is vulnerable to bow bugs, small beetles with a preference for horsehair. The bow bugs eat small sections of the hairs in the bow, and the remaining hairs spread out over the violin, creating a very chaotic appearance when the case is opened.

Violins are traditionally glued with a special glue that allows a craftsman to separate the components with a sharp blade. This glue will hold under a range of temperatures, but eventually extreme heat, cold, humidity, or dryness will cause the violin to become unglued. The ebony fingerboard may come loose, or the top lift off.

As the violin becomes unglued, parts may be lost. To an uninformed relative, the case and its contents may become a nuisance and suffer further damage as it's tossed into a bin of old relics. For reasons of sentiment, and the nagging feeling that the word Stradivarius on a label inside the fiddle might indicate some rare value, even though the complete label reads "Stradivarius, Mittenwald 1923," old violins are rarely thrown away.

Spring
Summer
Autumn
Winter

Just listen to that language: tuning pegs, strings going slack, bridges collapsing, sound posts falling, the rattle that increases as parts come loose, and then think of poor Mr. Shimerda, gone crazy with loneliness and homesickness, lying in his *coffin case,* there at the crossroads.

What is it about us that makes us search for a human face in the configuration of the moon's craters or in a knot of driftwood? It is one of the universal human activities. Walking the wooded draw west of our house, I passed a rotten stump with a face in its center. I am trying to remember just who I know who looks like that.

Everyone has at some time glanced up and noticed a cloud that resembles a face. Sometimes these occurrences are deemed to be miracles: the face of Mary appears on a chapel wall darkened by candle smoke, the face of Jesus floats up through the stains on an old linen shroud. And it seems a harmless activity when compared to all of the damage we do to the world in other ways, poisoning this and that, killing off one species after another. An apple that finds itself atop the body of a doll doesn't care that the doll maker has pinched its shriveled skin into the face of an old woman. The apple's black pips in the winy white core behind the miniature spectacles and under the little paper bonnet are still intent on sprouting apple trees. That star shape in which apple seeds are arranged suggests a grander destiny, one undeterred by meddlesome fingers.

Winter

He who goes for a day into the forest
should take bread for a week.

Walking our gravel road early in the morning, the sun so slow to rise into the silence, slow to ignite the pure fuel of the air. This is a morning like a roadmap, pink and blue, the destinations only lightly penciled.

Suddenly a crow shakes loose from a tree and flaps away cawing, five slow croaks like a frozen starter motor. Coarse frosty pastures, gray as coyote skins. A magpie, far east of its range, rises and falls with each deep wing beat – a black stone skipped across water.

A maple, bare now but which all summer bent heavily over its leafy shadow, can scarcely hold itself back from human happiness under the least touch of the breeze.

A dozen sparrows burst from a bush by the road, like somebody's name remembered after fifty years.

There's a starling walking the road, scolding himself in a scritchy kvetching voice. He seems out of place in the country, wearing an iridescent navy suit with spots of mud from a passing car, a purple silk neck scarf, and far too much oil in his hair. I have seen him before, walking the concourse at O'Hare in Chicago, dragging a cart of sample cases locked with silver chains.

From its nest in a conical heap of frosty stalks and sticks, a muskrat hears me stopping and sends a ripple of wariness across the pond and into the reeds beyond it. The hollow floods with watchful silence, as if it were part of one great eye. The muskrat waits. I turn a loud heel in the gravel and go on my way.

Along the western horizon, where the night has gone, there's a long white cloud like an opera glove – tiny pearl buttons all the way up to the elbow. And some neighbor came in the night in a hurry to borrow the moon and jerked it so hard from its nail that he left its thin wire, new-moon handle hanging in the west.

As winter approaches, I begin to get ready for the worst. You never know. I start up my gas-powered generator to see if it runs; I grease and oil my

1947 Farmall Cub tractor with its blade for moving snow; I put a box of kindling near the stove in my library by the pond. I check the pressure

tank in the well. I put the glass inserts in the storm doors. I make a warm place for the dogs. I want to be ready for bad weather. "It is easier to throw the load off the cart than to put it on," as my Czech neighbors might say.

You want to be ready for anything. My father once told me about a man in our town who had been purged by his doctor with caustic anti-parasitic potions and promptly passed a long segmented hookworm that the doctor displayed on the sidewalk in front of the man's house. It was summer, the weather pleasant, and for an hour following, the doctor, who apparently had nothing else to do, spoke to passersby about the dangers of going barefoot in places where pigs had been permitted to run.

Dad said the worm was about twelve feet in length, pale and gray like a long strip of soaked toilet paper, and had an ivory head the size of a baby's fist with a small sucking mouth surrounded by hooks the color and size of toenail parings. The sick man, recovering on a daybed on the sun porch, spoke through a screened window to people who wanted to wish him well and patiently answered their questions about how it had felt to have such a creature living inside him. You never know what can happen.

We were also cautioned about journeying far from home. As an example of the dangers, the town had a badly crippled woman named Lucy Tripp, who as a girl had traveled to New York City. As she walked along a sidewalk, sightseeing, she was struck by the outstretched hand of a suicide who had leapt from high above. Her spine had been shattered, and for the rest of her life, she was to walk bent forward at the waist, tapping the sidewalk with two black canes. Whenever the subject of travel to a big city was raised, someone would say, "Just remember what happened to Miss Tripp."

Two miles east along our road a family of beavers has dammed a creek and flooded a couple of acres of corn. The man who owns the land has tried to reclaim this part of it by pulling the dam apart, but the beavers

118

are better at repair than he is at destruction. So that part of the corn-field stands in water, unharvested, though the rest of the field has been picked.

The farmer has built a couple of small duck blinds next to the beavers' pond, thinking to get a little something for his labor, and he's camou-flaged them with a covering of corn shucks. Today he's turned his cows and calves in to the field to eat what's left of the cornstalks, and as I drove past, I saw two calves, one black and one brown, eating one of the duck blinds. The beavers and the cattle have the upper hand.

A cold morning. An old woman with a sweet shy smile – my Grand-mother Moser – is turning potatoes in hot fat, the thin slices bubbling and snapping and browning. The Second World War has just ended. She is using a small, bone-handled, three-tined fork, and she has been hold-ing it in the same hand and using it in the same way for so many years that one of the tines has been nearly worn away. Just as the fork is cap-tive to the old woman's way of frying potatoes, just as the fork is made to sweep her skillet in the same slow circles day after day, the old woman has been caught in the habits of my memory. Whenever I think of her, she must rise from her daybed by the parlor window and return to that hot kitchen and stand on her swollen feet at the wood range and begin frying potatoes. This is not the afterlife that the Lutheran church taught her to expect.

When I am gone, she will be freed from this duty. She has been stand-ing there in my memory for more than fifty years. Like her fork, my rec-ollection of her is beginning to wear down on one side. I can no longer see her as well as I once could, that is, from the fixed spot at the side of the warm wood range where I always stand and look up at the side of her face, the right side, with the pale brown birthmark in the hollow of her temple, under a loose wisp of gray hair.

My wife's great aunt, Helen Stetter, will soon celebrate her 107th birth-day. She lives in the Nebraska Sandhills, six hours north and west of the Bohemian Alps.

She is old enough to contain within her small head, with its steel gray curls and glittering eyeglasses, the memory of Sioux dancers coming down off the Rosebud to dance and chant on the main street of

her town, the dust on their bare legs streaked with sweat, their clothes in rags. In the year of her birth, old Chief Red Cloud, who had once had his run of the Powder River country in Wyoming, got arrested there for hunting without a permit.

When we attended her 100th birthday party, I made these notes:

> She is wearing a blue dress with a floral print and sits on the edge of her bed. She has scraped the frosting off a piece of her birthday cake and has set the cake aside until later. She says, my, she was frightened by those Indians. She says they were doing a "war dance," and she tests the effect of this by fixing her listener with her one good eye. It is a clear and intelligent eye that has studied the world on its own since, as a girl, she blinded the other with a needle while learning to sew. Because she has only one good eye, she has seen the entire twentieth century in just two dimensions, and her mind has come to regard most things in just two ways, black and white or right and wrong. When she talks, she holds one of her ancient freckled hands in the other and kneads the knuckles with her thumb. She is wearing a pair of leather deck shoes tied with rawhide thongs.

Someone may have told her that what she was watching from behind her mother's skirts on that afternoon was a war dance, but in the late 1890s, when she was a child, the great Indian wars were over, and the mass graves at Wounded Knee, seventy miles to the west, were already beginning to sink under the prairie grass. She was born after the hostilities had ended, but there was still enough blood and smoke in the air to have kept the fear of Indians alive in her for all these years.

Her forebears settled in the area near where Minnechuduza Creek runs into the Niobrara River. There was no town there then. Her father and two uncles made their living by butchering beef and selling it to the army stationed at Fort Niobrara. The three of them, young German-Americans, had come west from Virginia and had lived for a while at Sidney, where they sold meat to the soldiers at Fort Robinson. That had been during the 1870s, and they had probably been there in 1877, when Crazy Horse was bayoneted on the grounds, but she doesn't remember

the family speaking of that. Would they have spoken of that? One of her
uncles was a renowned storyteller. Surely he would have mentioned it if
he had been there to see it. He might even have bragged about being
there on that infamous day, for this was before a white man would have
felt shame at the behavior of his kind.

There are women like her in many families, ancient maiden aunts
who stayed home to take care of ailing parents, who have outlived their
brothers and sisters on the pure energy of bitter resentment. For nearly
a hundred years she has thought about the sacrifices she made so that
her brothers and sister could go on and have normal lives and raise families. At such an advanced age, she may revise her family's history in
whatever way she wishes, for she has outlived anyone who might con-
tradict her. In the past few years, she has begun to work her way back
through the family, singling out specific relatives to punish for ancient
slights and indiscretions.

She is not only the oldest person in her family but also the oldest
in the community. She is the sole living authority on not only her own
family but also the family histories of her neighbors. Not from her
but from published local histories, we know that in addition to his beef
business, her father was the proprietor of a tavern called the Deer Lodge
– a log structure built near the fort, where a soldier could buy a drink
and a woman. In his photographs, her father wears a rakehell handlebar
mustache, a wide smile, a broad-brimmed western-style hat, and a full-
length buffalo coat. To her, he is always "Dear Poppa, dear Poppa," delivered with a little sigh and a dainty dab at the corner of her good eye with
her flowered handkerchief.

Despite her occasional sallies against the long-dead, there is nothing
so spiteful about her that it can spoil her for us. She is the family miracle,
a true survivor, still strong and intelligent and borne forward into a
wonderful and strange new age.

Lots of people on the Great Plains pack up and go south from November
through February, but my wife and I enjoy winter in Nebraska.

Spring is downright impatient with people in their fifties and sixties:
we're under steady nagging pressure to turn over and plant a vegetable

garden, to gas up and check out the lawnmowers, to wait endlessly while the other party selects bedding plants at the greenhouse, and to begin the five-month-long, everyday chore of picking wood ticks off the dogs.

Spring
Summer
Autumn
Winter

Summer is one weary, endless, hot, dry mowing of grass, with interludes of garden weeding and chigger bites, and after every thunderstorm there are fallen branches to cut up with the chain saw and drag from one place to another. It is also the time when nature's weedy disorder reclaims the little bit of territory we thought we had cleared for ourselves.

Autumn is beautiful, my favorite season, with its clear skies and long shadows arrowing across the red hills, but it is also the time when the lawnmowers have to be drained and stored, when the pressure tank in the well house must be drained and checked, when the block heaters need to be installed on the cars, and when the dead plants in the garden must be pulled up and burned. It is also a time of sighing and regret, of the admission that during the spring and summer we didn't get done what we had hoped to.

Then winter sets in, and the obligations of our sixty-two acres are buried under the blessed somnolence of snow and ice. It is the time of lingering over suppers of meatloaf and squash and of wrapping ourselves in shawls in our chairs and reading books and nodding off at eight-thirty or nine. Then to bed under heaps of blankets and comforters, my wife in wool stockings, sweatshirt, and sweatpants, and I in the long flannel nightshirts my mother made.

Our food co-op has an aromatherapy display you pass on your way to the checkout counter, a couple of dozen attractively labeled vials: Essence of Pine, Essence of Wild Rose, Essence of Ginger, and so on. My Grandmother Kooser would have held up the checkout line while she stood on her broken-over shoes admiring these little bottles. She was a huge woman who enjoyed things miniature and perfect, and she kept rows of empty perfume bottles along her windowsills where they caught the light of the postwar 1940s. She lived in a rented house with rented but regularly dusted windowsills and was too poor to buy perfume for herself, but her friends gave her their empty bottles. I have what's left of her collection, and the three vials with the tightest stoppers still hold the faint sixty-year-old fragrances of Evening in Paris, White Shoulders, and one other scent so frail and delicate that it has irretrievably lost its name.

A person might be tempted to make fun of people who try to make themselves feel better by sniffing fragrances, but aromatherapy appeals to me. A familiar odor can fuel the fastest kind of time travel, speeding us back across the years.

But it's the unique combination of a number of fragrances into one indefinable evocative scent that punches its fist straight to the heart. I have been thinking this morning how many laboratory trials I would have to conduct, mixing test tubes of fragrances, to come up with that exquisite blend of odors that would take me back to a deeply pleasurable moment fifty years ago. There I was, standing in Sally Martin's kitchen, with my mittened hands stuffed in the pockets of my winter coat, when Sally took me by the shoulders and kissed me full on the lips, my first real kiss, a hot, soft, deep, wet kiss.

I can recall the smell of that moment but only guess at the ingredients: essence of boiling potatoes, essence of wet rubber galoshes, essence of sweat rising out of my collar, and the fresh celery smell of Sally's long brown hair. I would like to pull out the stopper of that lost bottle and be swiftly transported back to that warm kitchen on Kellogg Avenue in Ames, Iowa, in the first winter of the 1950s, snow puddling around our rubber boots set toe to toe on the linoleum, Sally and I at the beginning of long lives of kissing other people.

The electrician didn't like snakes, not at all. I thought I'd cleared them out before he arrived. I'd taken off the Styrofoam sheets that cover the pit, so the snakes would get uncomfortably cold and slither away. But when he pulled off the lid of the junction box, two snakes tumbled out, a two-foot blue racer and a three-foot bullsnake. He hollered, "I hate snakes!" and flew up the ladder. While he stood watching and panting, I went down into the pit, picked up the snakes, which were dull from the cold, and carried them over to the barn.

After he'd figured out what was wrong with the circuits and I'd paid

123

him and he was gone, I went to the barn to see if I could catch the bullsnake and blue racer and bring them back, but they'd already gone off to hide. I hope they can find a warm home for the rest of the winter. They certainly aren't going to try to make it fifty feet across the frozen ground just to get back into the well pit. They'd wind up like Commander Scott, who before dying of exposure left a plaintive note in his Antarctic journal, "For God's sake take care of our people." I'm doing my best.

We'd had two or three hard frosts, and there wasn't a sign of insect life anywhere outside, even though it had warmed up considerably as it often does after the annual Thanksgiving storm. I cut up a dead tree with my chain saw one morning and peered in under the loose wet bark, but there was nothing there but the abandoned meandering highways of whatever kind of bug made them. In the house, a few flies, slow and drunken looking, slapped the lampshades when we read in bed, and sometimes, early in the morning when I was wallowing up to my ears in the bathtub, a mosquito mysteriously appeared and whined in circles above me, baffled by the rising steam.

Besides the various kinds of spiders, welcome in our house, I discovered another insect that had decided to spend its winter inside. I would find it sitting motionless on the arm of the couch in the living room, watching me read. It had a tiny head and a broad flat back barred in shades of brown like a hawk or owl feather, and it looked like a painted African shield carried on the heads of four bearers.

Our insect book told me this fellow's name was the leaf-footed bug, a relative of the squash bug. According to the book, it was a predator, but I couldn't imagine what this one was finding for lunch in our house, which is usually clean and neat. He was more like a tiny camel, hopelessly trudging forever across vast deserts of plaster, no food or water anywhere in sight, condemned to never-ending exile.

Over the next few weeks I got in the habit of watching for him. I was attracted to his melancholy dreariness. All day he wandered up and down walls, across ceilings, like a cardiac patient walking a shopping mall. If sometimes I felt as if I were wasting my life, well, I always had the leaf-footed bug to show me things could be worse.

Occasionally, when suddenly agitated by some mysterious force, he would fly for a short distance, awkwardly whirring down the air of a room, to smack head-on into a wall on the other side. When the house was quiet, there would be a little click. The leaf-footed bug would fall to the floor, slowly gather itself as if brushing off its coat, and slowly move on. I was reminded of Harold Stassen, campaigning for president again and again. It was encoded behavior, I suspect, deeply imprinted in his genes, a complete disregard for failure.

This went on for weeks. I learned to expect him. Often, as I sat reading in the evening, I would discover the leaf-footed bug somewhere nearby, perhaps on the arm of the chair or on the nearby table, those tiny eyes watching me.

After several weeks, he was gone. I looked here and there but couldn't find him. He was not in the jungles of the flowerpots, not tracking the dust on the Venetian blinds. He was not among the dead and entangled daddy longlegs caught up in webs under the furniture.

Then, one day as I swept the floor, I found him lying on his back against a baseboard, his legs neatly folded over his breast. It looked like a stage death, like something from a melodrama. He looked like Count Dracula, pretending to sleep. Wake up, I said, you can't just give up like this. But he was gone, having floated away on the shallow little boat of his body. I swept him into the dustpan and was done with it.

But in the evenings now, when I sit under a lamp reading, the house darkened, I find myself searching the nearby furniture to see if he is out there in the shadows, watching me to see what I might do with my life.

I got out the Christmas decorations today, set up and decorated our little artificial tree, and unboxed and arranged the figures in the Kooser family crèche. Perhaps sixty or seventy years old and about the size and heft of a briefcase, it is made of thin hardboard splattered with plaster. When it was new, it was touched lightly with brown and rust-colored paints to make it look old. It is indeed a humble and even tacky setting for the birth of our savior, who lies with His pudgy ankles crossed and His hands spread wide as if to embrace the morning of His birth. All the figures are of cast plaster, enameled in primary and secondary colors. The

Savior's mother, a pretty young woman in blue with an open face, is down on one knee, hands folded in prayer. The adoptive father is down on both knees, his face pale and slack. He has the dark brown hair and beard of a man much younger than the Joseph of the Gospels, but perhaps the Gospels were wrong about this. Near these two stands an angel with broad thick wings and yellow hair. She blesses the moment by raising the broken-off stub of one arm.

Only two of the three kings have arrived, and both of them wear identical red robes and crowns that look a little like foil-wrapped kisses. Each carries in his hands a tall gilded box with a peculiar pyramidal lid, the kind of box that looks like a magic trick, that might have other smaller boxes inside and, inside those, even smaller boxes, designed to get a chuckle out of a baby. Two shepherds have arrived, wearing identical brown robes with wide-brimmed blue hats, which they have taken off to show respect (this courtesy has not occurred to the two kings, but they are foreigners). One of the shepherds has a very alert-looking lamb draped over his shoulders, so alert-looking that the shepherd can soon expect a warm trickle down his back. The other shepherd holds up one hand with his fingers folded around a hole about the size of the shaft of his missing crook. The crook has been deftly snatched from above by some divine prankster, and the shepherd has not yet noticed it is gone.

There are two donkeys, one standing wounded with a broken ear and another down on the hard brown floor, wearing a very sour expression as if terribly put upon. Another lamb stands alone with its head dropped, hoping the other shepherd will pick it up so that it too can have the pleasure of pissing down a human back.

The most unusual member of this group is a celluloid Jersey cow, orange in color and weighing so little you could blow it over with a good hard puff. How this cow got included among the plaster figures is a mystery. Perhaps my father, who was always in charge of the crèche, which once had belonged to his parents, decided that every stable needed a cow. Whatever the reason, it has a commanding presence. No matter where you place it, all the other figures immediately seem to arrange themselves in relation to it. Even the baby Jesus on his plaster cake of straw is upstaged by this cheerful-looking black-eyed cow, so light, so filled with a kind of airy joy right down to its bulging udder that it might at any moment ascend to heaven. Perhaps that's what the sour-looking donkey has been waiting for, some kind of a miracle.

❧

Few long-time city dwellers who move to the country for peace and quiet understand in advance how big an allowance of winter can get spent starting machinery, thawing plumbing pipes, or climbing down in a frigid well pit to puzzle over a sudden absence of water pressure at the moment your wife was ready to rinse the shampoo out of her hair. If a fellow has become accustomed to driving his suv into the local Firestone Car Care Center and tossing his car keys (with their lucky rabbit's foot) onto the glass counter, then striding out the door, topcoat flying, he probably has no idea what life is like in a drafty five-below-zero barn with cold feet and a runny nose, thirty miles from the nearest mechanic, praying that a fifty-year-old tractor will start.

We had six inches of snow on Sunday, preceding what the weather experts call an arctic air mass, but what I'd call a clear blue sky. That sky arrived this morning with a pale full moon in the west, lip-chapping winds, subzero cold, and a windchill of minus forty. Impassable drifts of snow blocked our driveway.

My 1947 Farmall Cub tractor was built prior to the invention of the windchill factor, and if it could scoff at such an elaboration, it would certainly scoff. Like other machines, it holds to the time-honored standard of mercury column temperatures. It was five below in the barn when I went there at six this morning to see if I could get the Cub to start. If I'd known in which of its orifices I might insert a fever thermometer, the tractor's temperature would have been precisely five below. In fact, I was the only thing within a mile that knew what the windchill factor was and was all the colder for knowing it. The radio had been tireless in re-minding me of it every ten minutes while I ate breakfast, and now I was being reminded of it by my puffs of breath, which hung in a sour coffee-flavored cloud before me. The red siding on the barn, the snowdrift at its door, the dusty glass of its little windows, every tool handle, every wisp of straw, all these were five below. Alice was as oblivious to the windchill as was the tractor as she happily snorted around in dark corners expect-ing to sniff out a rat, a long-dead sparrow, or some other delicacy.

The Cub has a five-foot snow blade on its front and a twenty-five-horsepower four-cylinder engine that can on a good day nudge a small heap of snow from one place to another. I hooked up the battery charger with its dial set to 6 VOLT START, checked the antifreeze level and the tire chains, squirted some ether into the carburetor intake (suddenly recalling a painful childhood tonsillectomy), said a short blessing, snapped on the charger, saw its arrow go over into the red zone, turned on the ignition, and cranked the starter. The Cub started right up, its little stack trumpeting an eye-burning flatulence of exhaust.

Spring
Summer
Autumn
Winter

I let it warm up for ten minutes, then folded an old blanket for the cold metal seat, sensitive as I am at my age to the caution that many farmers have picked up bad cases of prostate trouble from cold tractor seats, a rural variation on the germy toilet seats my mother had warned me about. I adjusted my cap, earflaps down, climbed aboard, and merrily lurched out into the drifts. I seemed the happy genius of the winter day, the center of our farm's attention. Every sparrow in the bushes, every field mouse in its burrow, every rat in the woodpile listened as I rattled to and fro.

Within an hour I'd gotten stuck and unstuck twice, lost my cap to a tree branch, torn up the end of our brick sidewalk with the tractor's chains, scraped a lot of gravel off the drive into the grass, given Alice reason to run in wild circles, barking, and burned a gallon of gas and a quart of oil. I had also created a high-speed bobsled chute in place of the driveway, which ascends to the county road and which my wife's Subaru had negotiated without any effort whatsoever while I was still tinkering in the barn. I also stalled the engine once, and since the battery wouldn't hold a charge and the generator didn't seem to work, I had to run a hundred-foot extension cord out from an outlet in the house, haul the charger from the barn, repeat my invocation, and start it again so I could steer it back into the cold silence of the barn.

I was able to accomplish all that in just three hours, and the guys at Firestone didn't get a cent of my money.

In addition to our standard Christmas decorations, tree and wreath and candles and so on, I've arranged some dollhouse furniture and tiny dolls on the floor in front of the fireplace. These were given to me several years ago by a friend. They had been hers as a girl, and they probably date from somewhere in the fifties. No plastic pieces, such as you'd find today, but solid wood. Refrigerator, stove, and sink, solid, heavy, and serious looking in thick white enamel. A bathtub and bathroom sink the same (toilet missing). These pieces modeled on the standards of the day, kitchen sinks with drainboard surfaces to either side, all of one piece and made of enameled steel, always cold under the fingers. Then there are painted wooden beds with mattresses, end tables, and a mirrored dresser and a chest of drawers with drawers that actually pull out. And the dolls. A family, with father and mother and two daughters, tattered and missing most of their hair. One of the daughters is in bed with the flu this morning, just as my wife is. The other daughter is sitting on the uncomfortable solid green couch between her parents, who are dressed for Christmas morning, the mother in a dress, the father in a suit. I set up a Christmas tree for them from my own belongings, one of those cone-shaped bottlebrush trees from the forties.

Spring
Summer
Autumn
Winter

This once was someone's dream of family life, a dream so badly tattered today. Worn out, bent, broken. On the faces of the dolls is an expression of astonishment at what the world has come to while they waited in the darkness of their cardboard box.

After I'd decorated our Christmas tree and arranged the doll furniture and set up the Kooser family crèche, I discovered the family reindeer were missing. When I was growing up, my parents had a set of eight white celluloid reindeer and another eight smaller, heavier ones made out of some kind of pre-plastic composition material painted in natural colors. These latter reindeer were antiques, I'm certain, from the turn of the century. They had once been on display in my grandparents' house. I was very much taken with them as a little boy because they looked so very real. They even had little bumps on their hard brown antlers that seemed authentic, though I don't know if real reindeer have such bumps.

Years later, after my sister and I were grown and gone, at about the time the entire country was in its antiquing phase, when people from coast to coast (including my mother) were trying to improve new pieces of furniture by making them look old and beat up, my father, then in retirement and always looking for something to do, got the idea to spray the reindeer gold. And he did. And then he put little necklaces of pea-sized red beads on rubber bands around their necks. I was disgusted. The white celluloid reindeer that had once seemed so buoyant looked heavy as hood ornaments, and the little composition reindeer, once so very real, looked like something you'd unscrew from the top of a bowling trophy.

Then, to add insult to injury, Dad glued quarter-sized cardboard circles on their feet, like snowshoes, because the reindeer had toppled over in the draft created whenever somebody opened the living room door.

Wanting to restore as much from my childhood Christmases as I could, I asked my sister by e-mail what might have become of the reindeer, and she replied that she was certain I had them. She said that when Mother moved into her assisted living apartment and we had given away most of her belongings, I had taken the reindeer home with me.

This afternoon I undertook a lengthy search, and on a shelf at the back of a closet, I found them in a yellow hatbox from my father's store, each wrapped in a brown tissue sleeve or yoke or collar from one of Mother's Simplicity sewing patterns. There aren't as many reindeer as there once were. Only one of the composition ones has survived, and the celluloid ones are down to five big and two small. I've just finished lining them up on top of the china cabinet, and they look as cheap and tawdry as the console radio that my mother antiqued pea green. But they do look like something from home.

It was eleven below zero when I got up at five this morning, and when I snapped on the light in the bathroom, I found a box elder bug stumbling along the edge of the tub. He looked discouraged, as if he'd spent the past couple of days looking for something to eat.

About a half inch long, slate gray with red trim, the box elder bug is known to rural Nebraskans, who are mostly Republicans, as the Democrat beetle, a nickname that originated at the time of the Roosevelt

130

administration, when Democrats were everywhere and into everything. And since we Democrats are presently grieving over the recent loss of the White House, perhaps my box elder bug has lost his patronage position in the Bureau of Wet Bark and Tree Sap and is looking for work. Or perhaps he's just beaten down by the insufferable smugness of Republicans.

Spring
Summer
Autumn
Winter

The University of Nebraska's Cooperative Extension writers put out useful reports on a variety of subjects from replacing light bulbs to changing the oil in your sewing machine. You can pick them up at the county courthouse, and I happen to have their four-page bulletin on box elder bugs. The paragraph entitled "Life History" begins: "In the spring, after emerging from overwintering sites . . ." Overwintering sites. I've always fancied a name for our acreage, but the suburban subdivisions have used up the really good ones, like Bonnee View and Pumpkin Glade. So at least for this one morning, with forbidding fields of subzero snow stretching in every direction, I intend to call our home "The Overwintering Place," a name that trundles over the tongue like a bug.

The bulletin says, "When seeking an overwintering site, box elder bugs often enter buildings through small openings around windows, doors, conduits, and pipes and through small cracks in or above the foundation." I'm not surprised by any of that, and we do have small openings all over the place, even one through which these small observations creep into my days. The bulletin goes on, "They do not damage food or other items in the home, nor do they bite humans or pets." Thank God, for, naked as a jaybird, I had stepped without caution right over this box elder bug and into the tub without a moment's thought that he might try to bite my belongings as they swung above him like the loader bucket on a dragline.

Since this is now "The Overwintering Place," I am prepared to extend hospitality to any and all box elder bugs, whose ancient race sounds so much like a clutch of uncles. In the autumn, the bulletin says, "activity continues well beyond frost as insects sun themselves on vertical walls on warm fall afternoons." How could anyone object to that? Fie on the Cooperative Extension Service, whose lack of charity comes through in the following sentences: "The best method of control once insects have

131

entered the home is to use a vacuum cleaner. If only an occasional bug is observed, a fly swatter makes an effective weapon." *A weapon?*

The Bohemians say, "An old man sees better behind himself than a young man sees in front of himself." I'm down in my pond-side library, next to the crackling wood stove. It's snowing lightly, and I've been thinking about Christmases past.

My grandmother, Grace Lang Kooser, was a large woman who spent most of her time in a favorite chair gossiping on the telephone. She was attacked one evening in the 1930s by a grapefruit-sized ball of lightning that leapt through an open living room window, burned its way across the floor to her feet, and vanished just short of the toes of her carpet slippers.

The ball of fire, which she said jumped up and down and hissed like a snapping turtle, had apparently followed the wire that my grandfather had hidden beneath the carpet as an antenna for his radio. One might wonder what made that fiery missile disappear at my grandmother's feet, but she was an imposing woman whose scorn was quite capable of stopping an act of God dead in its tracks.

The burnt carpet had been replaced long before I was born, and my grandfather had died when I was two, taking his radio with him, but the lightning ball lesson smoldered on in my grandmother's imagination. For the rest of her life, she looked with suspicion upon all electrical devices. She kept her icebox long after refrigerators had been introduced; she unplugged her toaster after every slice popped up; and she was especially wary of strings of Christmas lights. She had been a girl in the late 1800s, when Christmas trees had been decorated with real candles, and could remember stories in which trees had caused devastating fires. The fact that the bulbs in strings of Christmas lights were shaped like flames predicted danger. She insisted that my uncle Tubby, with whom she lived, set up their Christmas tree on an unheated glassed-in porch. If the lights should happen to ignite the needles, she reasoned, perhaps the firefighters could more easily save the rest of the house.

She also insisted that the tree be strung with oversized outdoor lights, which were presumed to be safer, having heavy wiring and thick black rubber sockets. This meant, of course, that the first thing one noticed about my grandmother's tree was the enormous bulbs with their red and green and blue coatings flaking away and the heavy tar-colored wiring under which the branches sagged. The wires looked thick enough to carry the power from Hoover Dam.

She had some lovely old glass ornaments, including graceful pheasants with sprays of feathery glass fibers for tails, pairs of snowy owls with glittering ruby eyes, and praying angels in fancy conical skirts. There were other glass ornaments in the shape of vegetables – carrots, turnips, parsnips. A few fruits and vegetables had been sewn from bits of cloth and stuffed with cotton – strawberries, plums, lemons, a few slices of orange. But you had to look very closely to identify any of these under the ominous cage of electrical cable.

My sister, Judy, and I sometimes spent Saturday afternoons with our grandmother Kooser. Because she was so heavy, she had difficulty moving about, and childcare was easiest for her if she could rest in her chair with us at her feet. From where we sat, her enormous legs swelled pale and white above the brown rolls at the tops of her nylon hose, and her knees were as large as the faces on Mt. Rushmore. She entertained us by reading stories aloud and scissoring the Des Moines Register into long strings of elaborate paper dolls.

When we got bored, we were permitted to explore the house. Grandmother Kooser had an ill-tempered black-and-white bull terrier named Fiji, who kept to himself on a rug in the kitchen. He was a great temptation to us, but if we got too close to him, he made a sound like a marble rolled across a hardwood floor.

On a window ledge above the staircase, so as to catch the light, she kept her collection of miniature glass bottles. She and my uncle had bedrooms upstairs, but all I can remember of them today is the big sagging bed in the shadows of my grandmother's room and the pungent medicinal scent of Lifebuoy soap that came from my uncle's doorway.

Maybe once a year, my sister, my grandmother, and I would make a "coal plant." This was a Mister Wizard kind of scientific experiment she'd read about somewhere, recommended for entertaining small children. The object was to create a thing of beauty from something as homely and common as a lump of coal.

133

I would be asked to select the object of the experiment from the dusty bin in her cellar and place it in a bowl. We always used a particular mashed potato bowl, blue and white, with little Chinese fishing villages around its base. Onto the coal we poured a mixture of household chemicals – I suppose it was made up of vinegar, baking soda, and food coloring. The objective was to create, through the formation of crystals, a miniature mountain covered with snow and forest. The lump was left to steep in this concoction, and by the time of our next visit, it would have begun to look not so much like a mountain as a lump of coal upon which a fuzzy, colored mold had formed.

During the days before Christmas, we would be permitted to press our faces to the French doors going out onto Grandmother Kooser's porch and gaze at the exiled Christmas tree, its strings of lights dark, its plug drawn far back from the socket.

Slowly, as Christmas approached, presents began to collect under the tree, a few new ones each time we came to visit. Those winters were cold. We children sometimes begged to be permitted to go onto the porch to squeeze and shake the packages, but we were ordered to put on our winter coats and caps to do so. Our breaths hung in puffs in the pine-scented air.

On Christmas afternoon, Mother and Father and Judy and I arrived at our grandmother's to exchange gifts. Uncle Tubby had plugged in the tree, and the huge outdoor bulbs glared, fierce pinpoints of white light beaming through their chipped colored skins. As he brought armloads of gifts from the freezing porch, his spectacles would fog over and he would wipe them with a handkerchief he had snatched from his pants pocket and snapped in the air.

We sat on chairs drawn into a circle in the living room, our coats over our shoulders because of the chill that had entered with the packages. As we unwrapped them, the paper popped like a frozen stream. If the gift were some item of clothing, a scarf or stocking cap, we would squeeze the cold air from it. Metal toys were beaded with moisture. The faces of my sister's dolls were covered with a light sweat of condensation. All of the gifts had to be set aside until they were warm enough to touch.

Once the presents had been unwrapped and a dessert of pie and ice cream had been served and eaten, my grandmother would signal my uncle with a nod, and he would promptly step back onto the side porch and unplug the tree. He would draw the cord far back from the wall outlet and coil it neatly next to the tree stand.

As we talked, the setting December sun would, for a few moments, touch our faces with a pale pink light, and then the living room would ease into darkness. On the marble-topped table by the window, the homely coal plant mercifully disappeared into shadow. My grandmother shifted in her chair, folded her hands on her lap, and sighed with satisfaction. Once again, her family had been spared from the flames.

🌿

We've had an ice storm. I knew a shy old man whose long hands swung from the cuffs of his shirts like the ice-coated branches sweeping our shadowy yard in the light from the kitchen window.

He was good with machines, but when his fingers were empty of work, he had no place to hide them. They never quite fit in his pockets. For more than eighty winters, he sat just inside the loose door to the world, watching his wife work in her kitchen. His fingers brushed a table there, feeling for something that ought to be tightened.

By the light of the kitchen window tonight, I see him out there on the threshold showing his hands to his wife, how clean he's got them, scrubbing them over and over.

🌿

In the weeks just before Christmas, my father's store was busiest, its narrow aisles crowded with shoppers, its carefully arranged displays rumpled and disarrayed, and its floors slippery with melting snow. On Saturdays and when school let out in the afternoons, my sister and I helped out. She worked on the sales floor, and I made bows for the women in the gift-wrap booth.

The bow machine was set up in the furnace room. A single light bulb hung over the card table upon which it sat. Behind my chair, the great gray furnace sighed and ticked, and piles of bald and disassembled manikins watched my back with wide unblinking eyes. In the shadows, bugs rustled across the floor, and above me the footfalls of customers knocked up and down the wooden floor. There I wound green and red satin ribbon into shiny bows that I dropped into a big cardboard box be-

135

side me. It was a job like those in fairy tales, in which a child is imprisoned in a castle and made to spin golden thread from flax straw.

Spring

Summer

Autumn

Winter

Occasionally, my dungeon-keep would be visited by Otto Uhley, the store's janitor. He was a friendly hump-backed man whose nose was runny from first frost until after Easter, and who frequently dabbed at his upper lip with the tip of his tongue. Because the bow machine was in his basement, he looked upon the bow making as his responsibility and included me in his rounds of mop closets, toilets, and shipping room.

As if to inspect my work, he would dip his great knobby hands into the bow box and swirl them about. The satin splashed and sparkled around his thick hairy wrists. Although it was my responsibility to deliver the finished bows to the gift-wrap booth, Otto liked to do it for me. Up the narrow back stairs he'd go, the big box in his arms, his round face buried chin deep in the shiny satin.

Sometimes, his visits to the furnace room would be cut short by the appearance of my father, who occasionally fled from the crush of customers above to stand for a moment or two in the quiet warmth of the basement. Whenever he came down the stairs, Otto would hurriedly scuffle off to the other end of the darkness under the store.

My father was then in his early fifties. As much as he enjoyed storekeeping, there were times when he was gray with fatigue. He often worked ten or twelve hours a day. As much as he liked visiting with customers, there were moments when he would fall silent and stare off into space. There were evenings when he would drive the family in our old Plymouth out to the edge of town, only to get away for a few moments. There, a farmer kept a pen of sheep, and my father would pull the car off the road and stop. "See, children," he'd say, "how much the sheep look like the people who come to the store. Why, look! There's Dr. Mason's wife, and Mrs. Fitch, and, oh, there's Gladys Fitzpatrick, bless her soul..."

It was at such times, when the press of the store had become more than my father could bear, that he would stop in the furnace room, his shoulders sunken, his arms hanging down as if to let his responsibilities drip from the tips of his fingers. Though he would have preferred to stand there in silence, taking a few breaths, he would ask me how the bow making was going and would answer questions about how things

136

were going on the sales floor above. Then, as quickly as he had appeared, he would be gone.

Except for these two visitors, I was alone. As the box filled with bows, my head filled with dreams. Behind me, the furnace breathed like an enormous and motherly old woman, pleased to have a boy among the dark folds of her skirts. Above me, the footsteps resounded with the spirit of giving. I could imagine women in rich furs, smiling and chatting, their shoulders sprinkled with new-fallen snow, their arms piled high with gifts, and upon each gift, one of my beautiful bows. I could imagine the presents spread about under the Christmas trees in their houses, each package lit by the winking lights. I could hear the rattle of the colorful paper as each package was torn open, my reverie enhanced by the rustle of the insects behind the furnace.

As the days drew closer to Christmas, the store became busier, and my box of bows was whisked away up the stairs before I'd had a chance to fill it. Sometimes, one of the women from the gift-wrap booth would come running down for it, thus spoiling Otto's opportunity to bury his wet nose in the gay colors. Sometimes, my father would come for the box, having passed by the booth in his endless rounds and seen that the women were nearly out of bows. The footsteps above me flowed together into a steady rumble along the wooden aisles.

In the evening, after the store had closed, my sister, my father, and I would pass through the aisles, finding the countertops in shambles and the floors a wet black swirl of grime. At the front door, waiting to let us out and lock up behind us, stood Otto, his nose dripping, his mop bucket at the ready.

And then, suddenly, it was Christmas Eve!

Late in the afternoon, I was told by my father that I could stop making bows. My work was finished. I shut off the light, put on my warm jacket, and walked snowy Main Street down to its end and back, enjoying the rush of last-minute shoppers, the Christmas carols being piped out under the awnings of the stores. I stopped to look at the animated display in the jewelry store window, tiny elves endlessly making toys in Santa's workshop. The cold air sang in my lungs. I hummed along with the carols as I walked back to the store. Christmas at last!

By the time the store closed that day, my father's face was gray and his hands trembled. He walked through the aisles, absent-mindedly touching the counters, straightening the loose piles of unsold clothing. Our

Spring

family was the last in the store. Even Otto had gone home before then,

Summer

his arms full of packages, the floor left dirty behind him.

Autumn

On the "Hold" shelf behind the counter in the gift-wrap booth would

Winter

be several packages, left by mistake, forgotten, big boxes and small, all mysterious in their gift wrappings. Thinking that someone might come for them, my sister and father and I would wait an extra half hour, standing at the front of the store and peering out into the darkening street, the diminishing traffic. But no one came back. Finally, we loaded the mystery gifts into the Plymouth to take them home, leaving a note taped to the door: "If you have forgotten your package in our gift-wrap department, you may pick it up at the home of our manager." This was followed by our address.

By that hour we were the only people in the streets, the headlights of the Plymouth searching the ruts in the snow. In every window, a Christmas tree glittered. My sister and I sat among the packages as our father drove home.

My mother met us at the door, and the smell of cookies baking poured out into the cold air. It seemed that every light in the house was turned on. The Christmas tree stood in the corner of the living room with packages spilling out from beneath it. We unloaded the strangers' orphaned gifts and put them in the entryway, leaving the porch light on to guide their owners, should they come.

Soon, my father's older brother, Tubby, would come to spend the evening. We would hear him coming across the snowy yard, ringing a belt of harness bells that had been in our family for many years. When he came in, the cold night air slid from his topcoat. His gifts for the family, left all day in the trunk of his car at his office, were like blocks of ice. We set them under the tree with the others and sat down together for supper.

All through the evening, as we opened our packages, strangers came to the door to claim their gifts. Uncomfortable, shy, apologetic, they thanked my father for taking the gifts home. As they stood in the doorway, snow melted from their boots onto the carpet and the cold air flowed in around them. What would they have done, they asked, how would they have explained to their children? Each of them glowed with good luck and gratitude.

Finally, all the mysterious packages were gone and all of the family's had been unwrapped. Our family gathered in the living room, which was lit only by the tree, my uncle Tubby dozing in an armchair, my father and mother together on the couch, and my sister and I stretched out on the floor below the tree, looking up through the glittering branches. It was quiet. Beyond the window, it was snowing. In a box in a corner of the room, the used Christmas wrappings rustled as they slowly unfolded. Near me, the shining bows sat in a little pile under the tree.

I've been watching my old dog, Buddy, as he gets ready to sleep by the fireplace. The way he turns and turns, then drops in a knot, is a lot like poaching an egg: with your spoon, you spin the boiling water, making a pocket, and then you drop in the egg, and it somehow holds together, a spiral nebula that loses no more than a few white sprays of light, just as in sleep each breath spins out and away from a dog, or from us, a slow subtraction that does not steal the peace we curl around.

I've been thinking this morning about the number of ermines you'd have to trap to trim Santa's outfit. An ermine is pretty small. The dogs killed a young one behind the barn several years ago, and it wasn't much bigger than a mouse. An adult ermine – actually a weasel in its winter snowsuit – can grow to ten inches long, excluding the tail, so after you'd cut off the head and tail and snipped off the arms and legs, you'd maybe have enough good fur to cover a toilet paper roll.

I did some fur trapping when I was a boy, and I think I'd use a small single-spring steel jump trap, baited with a piece of apple. If you tied the apple to the trigger plate with a piece of thread, you might save yourself a lot of lost bait.

You'd have to figure on losing some fur when you folded the seams in. I figure it'd take at least seven or eight of them just for the edge of his stocking cap and another couple for the ball of fur on the peak. Then you'd have to trim out the lapels and cuffs and hem of his jacket and have enough left to go around the tops of his boots. You might be able to get by with fifty or sixty full-grown ermine, but that could be a stretch, especially if you were tailoring an outfit for a good fat Santa. That's a whole lot of work. Even with perfect ermine habitat, you might find one or two to an acre.

❧

The Ben Franklin Store in Seward is going out of business. LOST OUR LEASE proclaims a long paper banner taped over the windows. I was told by a woman who works nearby that the owners of the building have tripled the rent.

Where will I go to buy those red Big Chief writing tablets with the wide school-ruled blue lines? Where will women buy checkered oilcloth for their kitchen tables? And where will people like my uncle Tubby go to buy boxes of cheap chocolate cherries to mail for Christmas gifts?

Freezing rain this morning, raw and cold. I've been sitting in Tubby's recliner by the fire that's in the wood stove, remembering another uncle, Jack Mayo, as he paid his daily visits to his big white tomcat, Fluff, who'd been exiled by my uncle's second wife, Crystal, to a chicken wire rabbit hutch on the side of the garage. An old man then, Uncle Jack would totter outside in weather like this, in his flannel robe and house slippers, to feed and water and console Fluff, who would look with a cat's cold haughtiness into my uncle's soft and homely face. Fluff had belonged to my late aunt, who had died a long and painful death from cancer, and though Crystal said Fluff's exile was necessary because he shed his hair on her furniture, our family suspected she didn't want my uncle cooing and clucking over anything my aunt had loved and cherished. I can remember Uncle Jack pushing a long finger through the wire to scratch Fluff's ears and the cat disdainfully tipping his head to better take advantage of this furtive love. That was more than thirty years ago and is as vivid to me as if I had just looked up to see my uncle slowly passing my kitchen window.

Now the Ben Franklin store is joining everything that's gone.

❧

I spend lots of winter days with books. I probably have the largest private library in Seward County, thousands of books. I can't resist them.

140

Writers are writers because they love to read. If I were to read two or three books every week, I couldn't live long enough to read through the books I own, but that doesn't keep me from buying more. Most of the ones I buy are from bookstore sale tables, but I've also found a number at thrift shops and garage sales.

I was looking just now at a stack of children's books. I collect them because I like to look at the illustrations. When asked, most writers will list among their literary influences great books like *War and Peace* or *Remembrance of Things Past*, but the most important influence on my writing and life was *Lentil*, a children's book written and illustrated by Robert McCloskey. It was first published by the Viking Press in 1940, and my copy was given to me by friends of my family while I was in grade school. In neat but labored cursive, I carefully inscribed the title page, "This book belongs to the Library of Teddy Kooser." I was already showing the telltale signs of the bibliophile I would one day become.

Lentil is the story of a schoolboy who, by what we in my family would call stick-to-itiveness, overcomes an inability to fit into the life of his community and becomes a local hero. It is no surprise that I identified with the protagonist. He was a boy about my age, ten or twelve; the author's wonderfully detailed pencil drawings of street scenes in the fictional small town of Alta, Ohio, looked much like my home town of Ames, Iowa; and the problem Lentil had in fitting in was a problem I had.

It's a simple story. Lentil occupies himself in the ways I once did, walking around town, up and down alleys, thinking about his place in the world. His main problem is that he is frequently embarrassed in the schoolroom because he is unable to sing as sweetly as his classmates. When he opens his mouth, he croaks. So he saves his pennies, purchases a harmonica, and practices it wherever he goes, hoping that by the sweetness of his harmonica playing, he will be redeemed in the eyes of his classmates.

The villain in the story is an old man named Sneep, the town spoilsport and sourpuss. Sneep doesn't like much of anything, and he especially doesn't like the town's most notable citizen, Colonel Carter. Sneep and Colonel Carter are about the same age, and perhaps Sneep, who has never made much of himself, is jealous of Colonel Carter, who is a wealthy benefactor and noted public servant. When the news gets out that the Colonel is coming back to Alta after two years away, old Sneep determines to spoil the celebration.

The townspeople deck out the town in bunting for the Colonel's arrival, and everybody gathers at the railroad depot to meet his train. A brass band has assembled, prepared to lead a parade through the streets. But Old Sneep gets on top of the depot roof and, when the train comes in, starts loudly slurping on a lemon. As a result, all of the band members pucker up, unable to blow their trumpets and trombones and tubas.

But Lentil is miraculously unaffected by Sneep's dirty trick, and he pulls out his harmonica and begins to play. The Colonel is so pleased with Lentil's music, especially his rendition of "She'll Be Comin' 'Round the Mountain," that he jigs a few steps on the depot platform and then lets Lentil ride with him at the head of the parade in his open touring car. All has gone well. Even Old Sneep is softened by the music. On the last page of the book is a drawing of Lentil, smiling, with the single sentence, "So you never know what can happen when you learn to play the harmonica."

When I was a boy, I felt a lot like Lentil. Surely the success of a story like his – I believe Lentil went through many reprintings – has to do with the fact that many if not most children feel they don't fit in. At that time I was small and awkward and no good at athletics, the true measure of acceptability in those days. I tried hard. I strapped on the football helmet my parents had lovingly bought me and got run right over as if I'd been a sandbag somebody had left on the playground. I couldn't run as fast, jump as far or as high, or talk the sports lingo as well as my classmates. I knew I'd never fit in. So I decided I'd have to find something I could do well if I wanted to be loved and admired. Inspired by Lentil, I bought a harmonica and tried to learn to play it. It was one of the Hohner "Old Standby" models, and though I practiced a lot, the only tune I ever learned to execute well was "Red River Valley." This modest accomplishment was never going to get me into the big parade.

I was better at drawing pictures and writing poems and stories, and eventually I converted my aspirations to becoming an artist and author. I had teachers who understood how important it is not to discourage children while they play with their crayons and pencils. They didn't tell me that my trees looked too much like lollipops or that my stories didn't end with a proper denouement. They smiled and patted my shoulder and ran their warm fingers through my hair. I know now that I was in the presence of the only angels we are ever likely to make the acquaintance of: teachers blessed with the love of small people who are trying to find their place in the world.

Some years later, during the summers I worked as a sign painter, I used to drive my old pickup truck into small towns in Iowa that were much like Alta, Ohio, Lentil's town, and set about to letter the glass windows of storefronts on Main Street. Old men would come out of the taverns and coffee shops, carrying folding chairs, and would sit behind me and watch me work. I was that exotic creature, an itinerant artist, and their attention and admiration warmed my back with a kind of bone-deep sunshine. There is nothing so pleasant as to have the admiration of those people we have come to call the locals.

But it was as a poet that I would finally become my own Lentil.

Because he was interested in writing and writers, Bob Kerrey, once Nebraska's senior senator, asked a mutual acquaintance to introduce us. This was in the 1970s, before he was to run for governor. He and I became fast friends, beginning an exchange of yarns and letters that continues today. When he was elected governor, Bob would occasionally drive out to our place in the country for a visit. He would dismiss his official driver, a trooper, and would himself pilot the official vehicle, a long black Chrysler or Lincoln, I forget which. Sometimes we'd go for a drive. We'd roll up and down the gravel roads, talking books and telling stories and laughing and raising a great plume of gubernatorial dust, and it came to me that there I was, at last, Lentil, riding in Colonel Carter's car at the head of the parade. *You never know* what can happen when you learn to play the harmonica.

This is the season for getting sick, and I have a cold.

When I was a freshman in college, I came down with pneumonia following a drunken tobogganing party. I was very ill, hospitalized for ten days and out of my head with fever for the first week. The walls and ceiling of my room took on a strange, softly undulating life that terrified

143

me. Once I saw glossy wet fur growing out of the grain of the wooden door. I later recalled having well-wishing visitors – friends and relatives – who in fact had never been to see me.

Spring
Summer
Autumn
Winter

As my fever fluctuated, I experienced brief periods of clarity and would lie with my sweaty bedding twisted about me, reading a book that someone had left by the bed. It was the only reading material in the room, a boy's novel about a German shepherd named King. Time and again, King came to the rescue of his blundering master. I knew that it was a book my intellectual college friends and teachers would sneer at, but my illness had reduced me to childishness, and as a child I fell for this simple, engrossing story. I was twenty years old, but because I was sick, I had regressed to half that age. I was completely dependent upon the loving care of adults – my parents, my doctor, and nurses. Near the end of my hospital stay, my sweetheart of four years came to my hospital room to tell me that she had found another boyfriend; I let her go without an argument, having been beaten back into a bemused, passive, pre-pubescent state.

The story of the noble dog, King, sustained me against the billowy craziness upon which my bed floated and bobbed like a raft. His story was richly detailed and absorbing. He made his way through snowdrifts, up and down the sheer faces of mountains, through flooded, ice-choked streams. King's adventures were breathtaking, marvelous, and like the faithful dog he was, he was always within calling range when his master needed him.

When my temperature finally went down and stayed down, I began looking about the room for the book, but it was nowhere to be found. My nurses told me that I'd been given no books because I'd been much too ill to read. When my parents came to visit, I asked them what had happened to it, and they said they couldn't recall ever seeing such a book. No one could account for the missing King.

But the book was vividly impressed upon my memory. I could still feel it in my hands and see its print in front of my eyes. It had to be there somewhere. I described it in detail: it had no dust jacket and was bound in red cloth frayed by wear; the binding was slightly sticky after holding it for a while; it was a little over an inch thick and had a comfortable, serious-feeling heft to it; the pages were of good prewar rag paper and had deckled edges; it had the good glue-and-ink smell of a book; the spine was stamped with the title in gold foil: King: A Dog of the North.

There were, of course, many such books in print at the time, the dog story being a staple of juvenile reading, and I had possibly read one or two of them when I'd been younger. But what I came to believe is that in my delirium, I wrote, printed, bound, and published King: A Dog of the North. I made it all up. Just as King, the dog, was always there when his master fell into the arms of a bear, King, the book, had snatched me from the jaws of pneumonia.

I have been a writer ever since. Oh, I'd written some poems before I got pneumonia, but it took pneumonia to make me serious about writing. The creation of King: A Dog of the North, a solid accomplishment of the imagination, may have given me the confidence to try my hand at letting my imagination carry me forward, toward other stories and poems and books like that one. And whatever success I've had as a writer, I owe in some part to that magnificent silver-haired German shepherd, who vanished into the frozen wasteland once he had seen me back to health. Writing late at night, sometimes I think I hear his great paws padding through the snow.

*

It's clear and quite cold, in the teens at daybreak, with a couple of inches of new snow on the ground. Icicles on the eaves troughs.

Because my sister told me today about a man in her neighborhood who is steeling himself for weeks of radiation of the neck, I got to thinking about a plumber I knew more than twenty years ago, a charming man who died of cancer, an inoperable tumor of the throat.

He and his wife had lived only in Nebraska for several years, having grown up in California. In their forties, they'd decided to try life in a new setting, and they'd blindly stuck a pin into a U.S. map and found Lincoln, Nebraska, where they had been very happy. I met him when I was remodeling and phoned for a plumber and liked him immensely. He was already ill and knew that he would die, but he wanted to finish his life as a plumber, using his skills.

His hobby was carving ice sculptures, and he had a part-time business making punchbowls and swans and angels for celebrations. He'd made arrangements with an ice company in Lincoln and could go there in his spare time to chip away at his creations, which he stored in their refrigerated vaults.

He died the summer I met him, and a few days afterward, I began wondering what would become of his sculptures. I drove to the ice company to ask what they intended to do, but they had already dismissed my friend's work, pushing the three sculptures that remained out onto their loading dock where they'd melted in the heat. I was told they'd been horses with wings.

Because a cousin I haven't seen for more than twenty years kindly answered my letter and sent me the recipe for his mother's molasses cookies, I should be happy. I should be making those cookies, savoring the strong, black, earthy odor of molasses, pushing the gritty white sugar into the lard, greasing the black tin sheet with Crisco, smearing it around with my fingers, pleased to have rescued her marvelous cookies from time. But because of his dried-out ballpoint pen that skipped as he held down the cheap lined paper, and because of his awkward, poorly spelled words and his confusion of tenses, present and past, and because his dear mother is gone, whom both of us loved, whom both of us wished would go on laughing and baking forever, and because the words for this come hard for both of us, I have been sitting a long time alone in my kitchen, not lifting a finger, with this recipe, a little scrap torn from oblivion, folded and then folded again, closed in my hand.

More and more frequently since I entered my sixties, I have begun to see my father's hands at the ends of my arms. Just now, the left and more awkward hand lies curled in my lap while the right one massages the beard on my chin. On the ring finger of the left is the silver wedding band that my wife gave me, not my father's gold ring with its little yellow sapphire. But I am not deceived; this wearing of my ring on his ring finger is a part of my father's respectful accommodation of me and of my life and marriage. Mine have succeeded his, which is, as he would have said, only as it should be.

I recognize his hands despite the ring. They are exactly as I remember

146

them from his own middle age – wrinkled, of course, with a slight sheen
to the tiny tile-work of the skin, with knotted branching veins, and with
thin dark hair that sets out from beneath the shirt cuffs as if to cover the
hand but that within an inch thins and disappears as if there were a
kind of glacial timberline there. There is, as we know, a field of coldness
just beyond the reaching tips of our fingers, and this hair has been discouraged and has fallen back.

As a young man, my father had been a drapery salesman in a department store, and his hands were ever after at their best when smoothing
fabric for display – the left one holding a piece of cloth unrolled from a
bolt while the right lovingly eased and teased the wrinkles from it, his
fingers spread and their tips lightly touching the cloth as if under them
were something grand and alive like the flank of a horse. I can feel the
little swirls of brocade beneath the ball of his thumb.

These hands have never done hard physical work, but they are not
plump or soft or damp and cool. Nor are their nails too carefully clipped
or too carefully buffed and polished. They are firm, solid, masculine
hands, and other men feel good about shaking them. They have a kind of
brotherly warmth, and when they pinch the selvage of the drapery fabric and work it just a little between thumb and finger, they do it with
power and confidence. There are pairs of hands like these – some brown,
some black, some white – in every bazaar in the world, hands easing and
smoothing, hands flying like doves through the dappled light under
time-riddled canvas.

I would like to be held by these hands, held by them as they were
when I was a child and I seemed to fall within them wherever I might
turn. I would like to feel them warm and broad against my back and
would like to be pressed to the breast of this man with his faint perfume
of aftershave, with the tiny brown moles on his neck, with the knot of
his necktie slightly darkened by perspiration. Now he has taken his
glasses off and set them on the mantel, and there are small red ovals on
the sides of his nose. I reach to touch them and find them wet, as if I were
touching something deep inside him. Now I hear him singing, softly
singing, the words buzzing deep in his chest.

But these old hands of his are past all that. They lie side by side in my

147

lap, their palms turned up as if to catch this fleeting moment as it falls away. But as I peer down into them, they begin to move on their own, to turn and shift. I watch the left hand slowly rise to place its palm against my heart and watch the right rise swiftly to enfold the other.

This book begins with an old proverb, "When God wishes to rejoice the heart of a poor man, He makes him lose his donkey and find it again." In the summer of 1998, I lost the donkey upon which I had ridden for many years, the ability to write. It was something that had given meaning to my life for forty years, and it was gone.

Nebraska had enjoyed abundant rains throughout April and May, and on Monday, June 1st, 1998, the city of Lincoln was lush and green. The temperature was in the low seventies. Perhaps this year we'd have a perfect early summer, I thought as I drove to the dentist's office, with enough moisture for the farmers and not too much heat for the rest of us.

The dental hygienist, a woman who'd cleaned my teeth many times, seemed clumsy and distracted that day, and as I sat back in her chair, I tried to divert my attention from the tiny injuries she was inflicting to the world beyond the picture window, where leafy treetops tossed in the breeze and above them a few immaculately white clouds loafed past, imprinted with swallows in flight.

When the hygienist had finished and I'd rinsed as instructed, she called in the dentist, a tall, cheerful, balding Nebraskan.

He tapped my teeth with his pick and peered around in my mouth.

"Could you take a look at the back of my tongue on the left side?" I asked. "I've had a sore spot back there for a number of weeks. It's probably nothing at all, but I thought I'd better have you take a look."

He wrapped a piece of gauze around my tongue, gently pulled it out, and, with his gloved finger, felt the area. It took him a couple of minutes, and I guessed he was thinking of what to say. "Well," he said, looking serious, "*something's* going on back there."

He turned to the hygienist, who had been looking on with intense curiosity. "Call over to the dental school and see if we can get Ted in as soon as possible."

The hygienist made an appointment with an oral pathologist while I sat there. She cheerfully kidded with the person on the other end of the line, saying she had "another tongue" that needed examining.

The pathologist was not able to see me that day or the following day, but I was able to see him on Wednesday. My wife went with me and
sat through the examination. The doctor was a small, neat, businesslike man who at first seemed rather distant but who warmed to us as he got over what we later decided was his shyness. He felt around the sore area and told me that it was probably nothing more than inflamed tonsillar tissue but that he'd like to biopsy it. He called in an oral surgeon and introduced us, and we scheduled the biopsy for the next day.

On Thursday the oral surgeon, a pleasant man with large but graceful hands, anesthetized my mouth with Novocain, and, with the help of a female assistant, snipped out several pieces of yellowish tissue. "Looks just like tonsillar tissue to me," he said, confidently. He sent me home with a prescription for painkillers.

With the help of the painkiller, I was able to get some sleep that night. I spent most of Friday in my bathrobe on the living room couch, reading a new novel written by a close friend. Then, early that afternoon, I got a call from the pathologist, whose voice was quiet and serious. I held my breath. "I'm afraid it's squamous cell carcinoma," he said, "both pieces of tissue I looked at."

"Oh, God!" I remember saying, in a voice that was partly a sob, partly a sigh. "What do I do now?"

He told me he'd already arranged a Monday appointment with a surgeon at the university medical center in Omaha, a teaching hospital. He said this doctor was a Sloan Kettering trained specialist in cancer of the head and neck. He'd already sent off a fax of his biopsy.

I phoned Kathleen at the office to tell her the news, and she came home early to be with me. I slept very little Friday night, sweating so badly that I soaked the sheets.

On Saturday we spent two hours with a therapist, trying to get control of our anxiety. He suggested relaxation exercises and gave me a session of hypnosis. Whenever I felt anxious or panicky, I was to proceed through a series of pleasant, orderly, imaginary scenarios. They involved envisioning a landscape, and I chose to imagine the scenic vista near my late grandparents' home on the Mississippi River in Iowa. It is my favorite countryside, and I have written about it all my life. That overlook, just off the highway, is probably five hundred feet above the river, and one can see upstream for at least ten miles and across into Wisconsin. There are always boats on the river, and I imagined these too, including a tug pushing a line of rusty iron ore barges north toward Minnesota. I imagined the smell of the cedars and hardwoods that grow near the overlook, of the ragweed down the side of the bluff, and of the warm limestone gravel upon which I imagined I was standing. I imagined a clear blue sky and a warm sun. On Saturday and Sunday nights I woke often but was able to get some sleep by imagining myself in that place until I drifted off. I came to rely on this scene for the next six months.

On Monday we met my surgeon, a pleasant but serious young man who examined me and asked if I did any public speaking in my work. He'd have to remove part of my tongue, and I might have a speech problem. "No speaking that I can't live without," I said. Kathleen interrupted and said, "But he is a poet; he gives poetry readings." By the time we saw him again, he had been to the public library, checked out my books, and read them.

Surgery followed. My doctor had expected the tumor to be early in its development, confined to the site, but he did a neck dissection to be certain it hadn't spread. It had, to the upper lymph nodes, under my jaw. He told me this bad news in my room at the hospital, recommended a full course of radiation, and then, when his clutch of young residents had moved into the hall, stayed behind for a moment. "I don't know what kind of spiritual life you have, Mr. Kooser," he said, "but you are about to enter one of the great life-affirming experiences."

Five days a week for six weeks I reported to a Lincoln hospital for radiation. My mouth erupted in sores that persisted for weeks after I'd completed the treatments. I could eat only milkshakes and Ensure. Each day when I came home, I stopped at the head of our lane and picked up a pebble from the road. I lined these up along the kitchen windowsill to count off the treatments. It took a lifetime, it seemed, to get to thirty. I dreaded waking up in the morning.

From the first of June 'til early winter, I was exhausted, anxious, depressed, and unable to write. I began taking a two-mile walk each morning. I'd been told to stay out of the sun for a year because of skin sensitivity, so I exercised before dawn, hiking the isolated country roads near where I live, sometimes with my wife but most often alone. *Spring*
Summer
Autumn
Winter

Then, as autumn began to fade and winter came on, I began to heal. One morning in early November, following my walk, I surprised myself by writing a poem. Soon I was writing every morning. Several years before, my friend Jim Harrison and I had carried on a correspondence in short poems. As a variation on this, I began pasting my morning poems on postcards and sending them to Jim. I wrote 130 poems during that winter, and a selection from these was eventually published by Carnegie Mellon University Press.

God had taken my donkey and helped me to find it again. You never know.

Next to a country road, in January, a string of Burlington Northern boxcars stands rust red against a clear sky. At rest like this, they have a steady tension, like the long bones of an old woman's fingers. The odd car, for there is always an odd car in a string like this, like the one dark kernel in every ear of corn, is on this bright subzero day red, white, and blue. Its paint is so fresh it looks sticky. *Columbia*, it reads, a lost word from America's past, a word like *liberty*, like *republic*, a word with the smell of black powder.

This car looks restless among the others, looks as if it were holding its breath. If it were free of the others, it would fly along the tracks under its own power, clickety-clickety, bending the dry weeds back over the snowdrifts by the force of its wild, free rush.

The Czechs say, "The longest journey is from the mother to the door." At the end of his childhood, a young man breaks from the hard tears of his family and follows his own way. Wherever he goes, he carries their name. After three or four generations, all of the brothers and sisters have scattered, and the sons of the brothers and sisters, and the sons of the brothers' and sisters' sons, each following the shimmering tracks of his own fortune. And the years fly by, click clack click clack.

Spring

Summer

Autumn

Winter

In a strange city, miles from his home, a man opens the phone book and runs a callused finger over the names of strangers. If they were ever here, the people of his scattered name, they are here no longer. Over the frozen railroad yards, white whistles of distance call. And into the new year, a hard winter of glistening steel.

Life is a long walk forward through the crowded cars of a passenger train, the bright world racing past beyond the windows, people on either side of the aisle, strangers whose stories we never learn, dear friends whose names we long remember, and passing acquaintances whose names and faces we take in like a breath and soon breathe away.

There is a windy perilous passage between each car and the next, and we steady ourselves and push across the iron couplers clenched beneath our feet. Because we are fearful and unsteady crossing through wind and noise, we more keenly feel the train rock under our legs, feel the steel rails give just a little under the weight, as if the rails were tightly stretched wire and there were nothing but air beneath them.

So many cars, so many passages. For you there may be the dangerous passage of puberty, the wind hot and wild in your hair, followed by marriage, during which for a while you walk lightly under an infinite blue sky, then the rushing warm air of the birth of your first child, and then, so soon it seems, a door slams shut behind you, and you find yourself out in the cold where you learn that the first of your parents has died.

But the next car is warm and bright, and you take a deep breath and unbutton your coat and wipe your glasses. People on either side, so generous with their friendship, turn up their faces to you, and you warm your hands in theirs. Some of them stand and grip your shoulders in their strong fingers, and you gladly accept their embraces, though you may not know them well. How young you feel in their arms.

And so it goes, car after car, passage to passage, as you make your way forward. The roadbed seems to grow more irregular under the wheels as you walk along – poor workmanship you think – and to steady yourself, you put your hands on people's shoulders. So much of the world, colorful as flying leaves, clatters past beyond the windows while you try to be attentive to those you move among, maybe stopping to help someone up from their seat, maybe pausing to tell a stranger about something you saw in one of the cars through which you passed, was it just yesterday or the day before? Could it have been a week ago, a month ago, perhaps a year?

Spring
Summer
Autumn
Winter

The locomotive is up ahead somewhere, and you hope to have a minute's talk with the engineer, just a minute to ask a few questions of him. You're pretty sure he'll be wearing his striped cap and have his red bandanna around his neck, badges of his authority, and he'll have his elbow crooked on the sill of the open window. How impassively he will be gazing at the passing world as if he's seen it all before. He knows just where the tracks will take us as they narrow and narrow and narrow ahead to the point where they seem to join.

But there are still so many cars ahead, the next and the next and the next, clatter to clatter to clatter, and we close a door against the wind and find a new year, a club car brightly lit, fresh flowers in vases on the tables, green meadows beyond the windows, and lots of people who, together – stranger, acquaintance, and friend – turn toward you and, smiling broadly, lift their glasses.

In the *American Lives* series